Staring at Dementia

Lessons from Mother

Danny E. Akin

© 2021
Published in the United States by Nurturing Faith, Macon, GA.
Nurturing Faith is a book imprint of Good Faith Media (goodfaithmedia.org).
Library of Congress Cataloging-in-Publication Data is available.

ISBN: 978-1-63528-138-5

All rights reserved. Printed in the United States of America.

All Scripture citations are from the New Revised Standard Version (NRSV)
unless otherwise indicated.

Parts of *Duncan Legacy II: Moving Mother: Transitions of Mother and Son*
are used with written permission by Duncan and Duncan Publishers, Bowdon Junction, GA.

Cover photo by Rebecca C. Akin.

Table of Contents

Acknowledgments
v

Preface
vii

Chapter 1: Independent Living
1

Chapter 2: Personal Care
21

Chapter 3: Memory Care
61

Chapter 4: Hospice Care
147

Chapter 5: Going Home
155

Acknowledgments

Becky, my wife and constant companion during this time, was immensely helpful in keeping me on track and providing wise counsel throughout the journaling and writing of *Staring at Dementia*. Becky and I were married just a few years before Mother moved about three miles from us to live at her retirement center. So, we all three were together for a long time.

Nurses, staff, directors, doctors, and chaplains were pleased to share stories that further defined Mother during her sixteen years in three units at the retirement center. Certain people were particularly noteworthy: Nurse Alicia was very close to Mother, especially near the end, perhaps partly because both women had three sons. Judy cared for and dressed Mother for some time and let me know when she needed more and larger clothes. Gina spent many hours talking to Mother, comforting her, and being a friend. All three of these women provided insights into Mother's character and enriched my description of her as she aged.

While I gratefully acknowledge the above persons for their stories and insights about Mother, the writings in this book come from Mother herself—stories shared during our visits and my continuous learning from her counsel and life experiences. What I learned in caring for Mother, including my anxieties and fears for her, my occasional anger at her, and my search to see her *self* as she aged, all came about because of the woman she was.

Mother and Dan: Best buds.

Preface

Mother retired. That was the word she used when she left her home and moved into a retirement center at age 82. Prior to starting this new life, Mother had looked after everyone else, so this move really was, in a way, retirement for her. She moved into a place where folks looked after her. Well, that is not exactly true. Mother continued to look after everyone—or tried to—*even when* she lived in the retirement center. She just did it in a different way. She was still Mother, but her address changed and gradually her life changed. So did mine.

I began a journal on Mother when she moved to be near me and my wife. As I kept up the journal, I noted how Mother changed and transitioned into her new life, first in an independent living apartment and later—as more assistance was needed—to a Personal Care setting and then a final move to Memory Care. The journal reminded me of her sayings, mannerisms, and philosophy of life. As I wrote, I thought about Mother's new life and realized that her transitions also involved my own.

When Mother began to suffer from dementia, she moved into what was officially called the Center for Alzheimer's and Dementia Care. Memory Care was the name used by staff and was the name printed on the front door of this new building. No one said "Alzheimer's" or "dementia." In the Memory Care center, Mother received around-the-clock care for all her needs. She was behind secure doors, and there was not much left of her independence—nor could there be.

I journaled many of our visits to try and capture the rapid and extreme changes occurring in her slowed-down life, with her memory and recollections shifting not only from day to day, but also at times from hour to hour. The journal became full of events, Mother's pronouncements, and the myriad of changes taking place in her life and mine. This once competent, "could do it all" woman began to depend upon me for her decisions. While her living experiences of the past held true, her recollection of events became faulty. Our roles changed, and eventually I became the parent.

While some of Mother's changes were uniquely her own, there were some general declines in her health that aligned with a diagnosis of dementia. Everyone involved in Mother's care tried to be cognizant of these declines and plan her moves accordingly. And with Mother's uncanny knowledge of herself, I think we were generally successful.

Writing about these times, particularly during the most stressful episodes, gave me a sense of purpose even as I struggled to make sense of difficult situations and decisions. As I look back and remember my feelings of frustration, there are times when I regret my anger—even when I tried to see the humor. Wise advice from other writers prompted me to look for the *self*, the person that remained of the mother I loved. Often, I found it in her kindness and even, at times, in her words.

Caregivers—particularly if they are family members—go through transitions with the person being cared for. While Mother's transitions were of interest to me, being the youngest of her three sons, her experiences also have meaning for others who are traveling this road. My life changed immeasurably, and her care was more than just a part of my life, it was my job. As I became more involved with this new job, I realized I was transitioning from my role as son to that of primary outside caregiver.

So, why did I write this book? I did so mostly because I want to share the legacy of Mother, a woman who, without fame, wealth, or status—at least as the world defines it—deeply influenced the lives of her sons, grandchildren, great-grandchildren, extended family, church, neighbors, friends, and retirement home staff. I want to recall the *self* still present in this selfless saint. However, I also want to relate Mother's transition to dependence and mine to caregiver and confess those feelings—joy, anger, frustration, love, humor, and amazement—that a caregiver experiences during these transitions.

It is my hope that this book will give others who must travel this road some hope, practical advice, a feeling of camaraderie with fellow caregivers, humor, and the encouragement to write down the stories of their parents before the stories are lost forever.

Chapter 1
Independent Living

Life Was Good ... Until It Wasn't

... 56 years: That's how long Mother had lived in the same house before she decided it was time to move into a retirement center. She and Dad had built the small house in the midst of World War II and expanded it as the family grew to include three sons. She enjoyed the home and its trees, or the "grove" as we called it, and the big vegetable garden that provided us with jars and jars of green beans and tomatoes for the winter. We three sons went off to college, got married, and lived far from home and Mother. She took care of a sick husband for many years, and then maintained her home alone after Dad died ten years before her move. But cracks had begun to show in the old home place, both literal and figurative. The house needed considerable upkeep and maintenance, and those worries "got into bed with her"—to use one of her classic phrases.

Not only that, but the family Easter gathering Mother had hosted a few months before her move proved pivotal. Many of her children and grandchildren descended upon her house, some staying overnight. As she had always done before, and as expected, Mother did it all: cleaning, cooking, and hosting. Some family members tried to lighten her load by offering to bring food, but she pretty much hosted Easter alone. We thought she wanted it that way. I had

Mother preparing a huge family meal in her kitchen.

suspected for a while that hosting big gatherings was getting to be too much for her, and that Easter proved me right. It took Mother a long time to recover. She seemed to realize, perhaps for the first time, that she could not do everything she used to do—and, more importantly, she did not want to do everything she used to do. For the first time that I could recall, Mother said, "I will sell the house and move to where someone can take care of me."

Another event, which I did not know what to make of at first, clinched the deal for Mother. While talking about her impending move, she told me: "I heard just as clear as if he was standing next to me. Your Dad said it was okay for me to move and start this part of my life." I now know that such experiences are not uncommon. Once she had received Dad's blessing, Mother never second-guessed her decision to sell her house and move. She never looked back. She did not keep up with old neighbors; she never saw her house again; she sold her car and never drove again.

Mother had always liked to make her own decisions, and so it was with this one. For a woman who did not like change, Mother's decision to sell her house and move was bold, a bit unexpected, and very welcomed. To be clear, it was Mother's choice to move to a retirement center, and Mother's sons knew her decision was a godsend.

I do not remember having discussions with anyone about the financial considerations of Mother's move. Mother lived frugally on her Social Security, the little money that she and Dad had saved, and through crafty buying, doing for herself, and not much else. She was extremely frugal and did not like handouts, even from her sons. Mother had the noble, down-to-earth, make-it-work character that resided in the ordinary men and women Tom Brokaw so elegantly profiled in his book, *The Greatest Generation*[1]. While Mother's lifestyle began out of necessity, it became for her the preferred way of living well on as little as needed. Mother had enough, though, and I never remember her complaining of having too little.

Her frugal way of life came not only from living on the farm with her mother and father in the 1920s but also from her fifth-grade health book, *Everyday Living for Boys and Girls* by Maude Calvert.[2] A few of Mrs. Calvert's financial rules to make it in the world were: "Much of the unhappiness, most of the poverty and a majority of the failures in the world are caused by lack of thrift; thrift deals with little things and can be practiced by everyone, but it requires willpower; there is only one way to earn money or anything else, and that is by work; by saving only a part of each year's income, it is easy to lay up sufficient to be independent in old age." Mother followed this advice.

Further, I cannot remember any discussion with doctors about Mother's health prior to her move. Since she had no medical concerns, except her eyes and a loose tooth from a fall (she had previously recovered from a broken hip and subsequent operation), I am not sure that Mother or any of us thought much about, or saw the need for, doctors at this time. Likely, Mother felt confident the impending move could be handled without fuss about such medical matters. After all, she was in great health and only 82! "Things will work out," she said.

Independent Living

Dan learning from Mother how to bake her signature coconut cake.

Mother chose a retirement center 120 miles from her old home and about three miles from the home of my wife and me. I had in mind another center close by—a newer, fancier one, but Mother just seemed to know the right one for her. The center was nestled among the trees and away from the main highway, unlike the one I suggested. She chose it not knowing much about it, I thought, but Mother chose positively and without hesitation. Her choice was a wise one. As we later found out, Mother's decision on where to move was the second godsend.

In reflecting on Mother and her attitude, I realized that I, and others in her family—and some granddaughters in particular—share a similar trait: Once we have completed something, whether finishing school, quitting a group, or moving, we do not look back. We do not keep trying to be a part of the past. We move on. This was Mother too.

Mother worked at making a new life for herself in independent living. After some initial fear over leaving her home, she began making new friends and visiting around more. She made a list of everyone's names and learned about her neighbors. She shopped with the other ladies on senior grocery shopping day, and when the time came for a walker, she got one in the same style as the other ladies. She even wore pants just like the other ladies. This was particularly surprising because Mother had only worn pants to pick huckleberries. Now she *only* wore pants. Mother adjusted well and enjoyed independent living. It did not take her long to enjoy having her meals cooked and dishes washed and no house repairs or grass-cutting to do. Someone else was taking care of her.

Living close by, I could now visit Mother and talk with her, learning more than I knew before about her early life with her growing-up family. Her mind was sharp in recounting her parents (S.B. and Belle) and her eight siblings: Amon, Ira, Alera (whom everyone called

Lilly), Eugene, Bernice, Audie and Aubrie (twins), and Mildred. (Mother was second from the youngest.) I took her to doctor and dentist appointments and sometimes to stores, being sure not to intrude on senior grocery shopping days with the ladies. We visited, told stories, laughed, and sometimes got miffed with each other. With her consent and help, I even learned to bake her signature coconut cake that had been a favorite at reunions, birthdays, and other celebrations.

Life was good ... until it wasn't.

Who's in My Bed Tonight?

"It's someone different every night," Mother told me at one point. "Always a family member. Sometimes it's a sister, and sometimes it is *you*."

This was new. I asked her if it was scary for her.

"Not at all. It is comforting to have family near me," Mother responded. Mother said that most every night she had this feeling of someone with her: "Last night it was three babies. Two were great-grandchildren, but I do not know who the third baby was," she happily recalled. A granddaughter and mother of two babies had recently visited, so likely the people she felt were with her that night came from this contact. Coincidentally, a few days later we found out that the granddaughter was expecting a third baby. At times I thought I saw an event that prompted these phantom visits, but at other times I could find no connection.

A few years into her independent living, a brother and I noticed significant behavioral changes in Mother. We euphemistically explained it as Mother being "not at the top of her game." I had observed that she was not as interested in our conversations as before. She often did not hear the conversation and did not seem to make an effort to connect with me. This was in contrast to a short time earlier when she had wrestled from her reticent son the price of a land deal. Now, however, it seemed as though our talks did not matter, and while the subject really might not have mattered, it was the change in Mother's behavior—her disinterest—that concerned us. She complained of not having much to do, especially on Sundays when many events took place. She could not remember dates. Most telling, however, was that she did not record her bank checks as she had meticulously done before. We did not know if these changes were temporary, or if they signaled a bigger issue for Mother, and for us.

Mother's troubles became more apparent after six years in independent living. Ironically, it began on one of the highlights of the year: the 50th wedding anniversary of my older brother and his wife, which was held at the location of their ceremony near the beach. Worried about the possibility of Mother having to cancel an expensive room at the last minute, I booked one room for my wife, myself, and Mother. While the plan was solid (I thought), my wife and I both learned a lot about Mother those two nights, including what she did during the day, how she got ready for something, and her desire for no air conditioning in the hot, humid August weather.

Mother showed some signs of mental decline, such as confusing families. While these little snippets were telling, the most striking revelation into Mother's mental state occurred on our

Mother with her three sons standing outside her home of 56 years as she prepares to leave for the retirement center.

trip back home. Mother woke from a nap and was insistent on knowing the roads, how far from home we were, and how close we were to her hometown (where she was born). After several rounds of questions, it dawned on me that Mother was trying to find a focal point. She felt lost; she did not know where she was. Our concerns intensified when we arrived at her apartment ... which she did not recognize. Her lostness was about more than not knowing her location.

Another day trip further worsened her mental fatigue. Although she recovered after a few days from making odd statements such as about who was or was not present, minor annoyances—including problems with the television—sent Mother into a panic. She was apologetic at her state and expressed what became a familiar refrain: "I used to be able to do all these things. I do not know what is wrong with me."

Mother suffered with lack of energy and some hoarseness, so I took her to see her doctor not long after the beach trip. Explaining the symptoms of Mother's illness proved difficult. Other than the obvious symptoms, everything else was murky. Mother described it as a "dullness" in her mind. One conversation between Mother and the doctor stuck out to me as symptomatic of Mother's concern about herself, her loss of self-confidence, and her confusion. She asked, "Doctor, can I hear out of my left ear?" I watched as the doctor was silent for a moment, assessing this question. The doctor then replied that more tests would have to be done to determine the answer. In reality, Mother simply wanted to know "what is happening to me?"

Mother's memory continued to decline. She even forgot devotion time with the pastor who came once a month after dinner to the retirement center for scripture reading and the

Lord's Supper. Close to this time of her decline, I came across the writings from a Sunday School lesson about the nation of Israel when captives from the ancient kingdom of Judah were taken to Babylon about 586 BCE. The author, Katheryn P. Darr, explained, "Order and control were undoubtedly important issues for a community who had experienced loss of nation, dislocation, and captivity." Darr used the new temple vision seen by the biblical prophet Ezekiel to show symmetry, precision, and regulations. She continued, "Ezekiel's vision constructed a world with its own internal and carefully controlled order ... where God's people could experience security born of clear boundaries and unwavering obedience to God's instructions."[3] This was Ezekiel's hope: the restoration of internal, controlled order.

This story struck me as analogous to Mother's situation—the loss of her internal, controlled order and her need to restore it. She had always been a person of boundaries, of internal and controlled order, but her current mental state confused and disrupted order, stability, and control. Mother recognized the loss in herself, and the litany of questions she asked after waking in the car on the return trip from the beach was a recognition of her loss and her initial effort to restore order and control. Mother's situation was a shock to all of us. The path forward was not clear, as neither Mother nor I knew what to do.

In time, Mother seemed to recover from her "dullness of the mind." After a few days' rest, she began to function well and seemed to restore order to her life. An antibiotic her doctor prescribed probably helped. She could remember all her friend's names, even the social director. We relaxed for the moment—but just for a moment.

Troubles Continue

I began to realize that Mother's disorientation on the return home from the beach was not a singular event. A few weeks after the return, and after she began to show some normalcy, she began to complain—almost obsess—about feeling lonely and sad. She said again that there was not much to do on the weekends; there was nobody around. She was in a depressed condition almost every morning. The sad feeling left her at some point during the day, but the depression was soon back again and seemed to occur every day.

The doctor gave her a mild antidepressant, and she began to take half a pill (5 mg) daily. It would take a few days for her to feel an effect from this medicine, I was told, but Mother seemed to put a lot of emphasis on it keeping her awake the first night. In fact, I was somewhat at fault for this, since I had told her to take the pill before bedtime. Even though it was a very low dose, the effect should not have been felt for some days, and the pharmacist had recommended taking it at night because of drowsiness. Mother, however, did not think it a good idea to take it at night, so she decided to take the half pill in the mornings.

For days thereafter, Mother and I had confusing and troubling conversations. Mother would combine two conversations, shifting between the two, and inserting folks from one conversation into the other, finally letting one conversation slip away. Her mental state seemed to be deteriorating, but I was still hoping for the restoration.

Mother was very aware that things were not right. We talked a lot about why she felt as she did, and she asked repeatedly why she was this way and what was wrong. My brother reported that he had had the same conversation with her earlier. We decided on a course of action of reassurance that she would improve and the medicine would kick in soon. At this point, we had scarce little else.

What Is Mother's Mission Now?

Mother's boundaries and internal controls had always guided her and were demonstrated in her actions. Over the years, her life had revolved around the practice of her faith and on Sundays being in church. But with her move to independent living, she did not want to join a church, even my church. Now without a car, maybe she did not want to "be a burden" on anyone, or maybe she wanted to do things her own way. Or perhaps she figured she had gone to church long enough. I was not sure. A kind deacon from a local Baptist church came every Sunday to Mother's place and taught a Sunday School lesson. This became Mother's worship time with others.

The hours were many, however, that Mother and I talked about her ministry *now*—how she could serve and be useful. We concluded that her ministry now was very local and limited to the residents and staff of the retirement home. She could practice her lifelong beliefs where she was. She could show kindness, consideration, and help to all she met, and by all accounts, she did and did so humbly. Everyone spoke sincere words about how Mother always treated everyone with kindness and consideration. She proved she could live out her faith wherever she was.

With her limited abilities and the restrictions of the retirement home, Mother's ministry might have also seemed limited. On the other hand, the Jewish prophet Micah in the 700s BCE related what was expected of Mother: "He has told you, O Man, what is good; and what does the Lord require of you, but to do justice, and to love kindness, and to walk humbly with your God" (6:8).

Wasn't this what Mother was doing all along, living out the words of the prophet Micah? Despite Mother's constant loving, humble attitude, her life was about to get more difficult.

Alzheimer's Disease

The first week of September was pivotal. Mother complained of feeling lonely and sad and had no interest in activities. After a few days of the antidepressant, she was also extremely confused, so I stopped the medicine. The next day, Mother experienced a quick and steep decline.

The last thing Mother remembered, she said, was leaving bingo. She had gone to dinner as usual, but she could not get back to her room. A tablemate brought Mother to her room and called me. I left a meeting and went to her room, where I found her very confused and wearing shoes of different colors.

I was able to take her to her regular doctor the following day. The doctor began a series of questions to establish Mother's mental situation:

"What year it is?" the doctor asked.

"1954," Mother replied.

"Who is the president?"

"Nixon."

The doctor then began what I found out later was a standard test for mental state. He told her, "I will tell you three words—apple, penny, table—and you repeat them later when I ask for them." When asked, Mother turned to me for help.

Mother's problem was due in part to low blood sodium. Her blood profile showed a sodium level significantly lower than the normal range that could cause confusion. Her doctor arranged for an MRI of her head and a visit to a neurologist. The MRI did not show any cancer or stroke. Both her regular doctor and the neurologist attributed the quick memory loss and confusion to abnormally low blood sodium, but they *both* also indicated other cognitive problems. For the first time we heard "Alzheimer's Disease." The neurologist thought Mother was in the early stages of Alzheimer's.

Either because of shock or wanting to hear it plainly put, I asked the neurologist, "Are we in a life change?"

"Yes."

Part of the transition we were to experience was that Mother could not live alone in her apartment. Thus, my two brothers and I began rotating overnight stays with her. During these times, we could not believe how much Mother had declined in such a short period. At times, she just stared and then tried to figure out her situation. I heard her pray for God to help her.

Mother knew she was not mentally stable. She knew she could not remember or function as before. She tried to go back to what had always worked, which was to work it out or "will it to be so." But this time she could not—and she was totally frustrated.

During the two worst weeks of the low sodium effects, there was a constant litany of laments: "I have got to find myself. Do you know about me? What happened to me? Does everybody know about me? When did it start? What happened to me? Do you know about me? Does everyone know about me—that I'm crazy. Did I do anything foolish?" Then, she summed it up pretty well: "I am so confused I do not know what decisions to make or not to make." And perhaps, most prescient: "I am here, but I am not here." At her worst, she would say with fear, "I am going to die." I was not ready to hear Mother say she was going to die. Her statement, which she made more than once and always in fear, made me wonder if anyone is ever ready to die, despite faith.

We knew Mother could not stay alone. We knew she would have to move to where there was more care, but we could not find a place with additional care at the time. I put Mother on the waiting list for a room in the adjacent Personal Care. We set up a schedule where my two brothers and I alternated staying with her for one to three nights at a time. I am not sure how my brothers maintained their sanity—or even if they did during their stint. For me, and to try to relieve my tension, I alternated strategies, none of which worked very well. I tried to be conciliatory, firm, stern, and even harsh when I lost patience. I then felt guilty that I was not patient or kind enough. Mother's hovering was particularly annoying. She had constant need for attention, and she quickly got into a habit of having everyone do everything for her. I was surprised because before Mother was the one always doing for others. She talked about herself constantly, usually with the preface that "I do not want to talk about myself."

My "Mother duty" times were not pleasant, and I imagined neither were they for my brothers. I would try to establish my ground and argue with or correct her. I felt as if I was an adult with a child who was not making good decisions. I realized soon that a lady of 90 years, even with dementia, has worlds of experience on me—experience on getting her way. She was adept at beating me down, so I would give in to an idea (such as dropping some medicine because she complained about taking too much medicine), but—and this was a long-held characteristic of Mother—it was not enough for me to permit; I had *to agree* to it. When pushed to the brink, I would give in or correct her. I did both, not feeling good about either way. I struggled to establish a comfortable foothold in this new relationship. Like Mother, I had never been here before.

Of all things, my electric toothbrush became the flashpoint. At Mother's apartment my electric toothbrush was cutting out and not recharging properly. I had cleaned the base and done everything I could think of to fix it. At some point, however, I discovered the problem: As Mother became disoriented, she would wander about her apartment, moving things, putting things away, and unplugging them. The following morning, I noticed my toothbrush charger was unplugged. Then, the next morning I found she had taken the toothbrush off the charger. I moved it to the kitchen for safety, but she unplugged the charger again the next day.

Frustrated, I said harshly, "Don't unplug my toothbrush again. You did it three nights in a row." I did not feel guilty. Mother responded that I should not be impatient or cross with her. I foolishly retorted that we had two people here trying to live together. In my mind, it was not working so well.

I just did not understand the disease or how to cope. Mother had never been like this before.

As predicted by the doctors, she began to improve in a few weeks as her sodium levels increased, but she was still very self-centered. Improvement meant there were good days mixed with confused days. But she *was* humming again, a characteristic that defined Mother but that she had recently stopped. Often, she wanted my attention to explain herself. At one point, she began to express her thankfulness and how wonderful everything was. While there was some lifting of the dullness of her mind, a "willing of things to be" crept in. I think Mother felt she was gaining some control of the situation, whether real or not. She was sickeningly expressive of her sons and how wonderful we were. I did not feel wonderful; I was just a son who loved his Mother and who was trying, under very trying times, to care for her. I certainly did not feel I was patient.

I went back to a strategy of maintaining a stern—not cross—attitude to counter and survive this too-happy attitude of wonderfulness. After the umpteenth rendition of "It is so wonderful to be back. Do you know what happened to me? You do! How long have I been that way? Did I do anything foolish?" I tried to interject a modicum of restraint and information. My strategy was to state and restate at every opportunity that she had a medical condition caused by low sodium in the blood and probably brought about by some medicine. "This condition is not common," I would tell her, "but does happen at times and when it happens there is memory loss and confusion. You are getting better."

I guess I did not know my Mother as well as I thought I did. Surprising to me, Mother was quite concerned about what people would think. Early on, she felt the need to fit in and be like the other ladies in independent living by wearing pants and having the right walker. Maybe she had always been this way, and I just did not know it.

Two weeks passed, and Mother began going to dinner and playing bingo again. There were good days and bad days, but there was always a lot of talk about herself. She would often say the Lord had told her particular things. For example, God told her she needed more care and that it was time to move to a place for this, which was reminiscent of her move from home to the retirement center. She mentioned the need for a woman to care for her, but some days Mother was so clear that I wondered if she needed this next move to Personal Care. But then I was thrust back to reality by her lost watch, lost bedroom shoes, and lack of knowledge of her medicine. And my toothbrush was still unplugged at night.

It was clear we needed help. Good fortune smiled on us as a member of the staff in Personal Care asked about a few hours extra work. She had good recommendations, and we jumped at this opportunity.

As we moved into autumn, Mother continued to make progress. She focused less on what had happened to her, and we continued to talk positively about a move to Personal Care. In fact, I think she began to make the transition herself. Mother began going to the nurses at Personal Care for items and to check things out. I even asked her to go to Personal Care for her medicines after dinner for a short time. Despite some recovery from the extreme memory loss and confusion, however, there were still times when she was utterly confused as to where things were and what to do next.

As long as the procedure was to follow what had been done many times before, she was able to perform. But when a new action was added or she had to connect thoughts and come up with a plan, she failed. As we moved through the next few weeks and her blood sodium levels returned to normal, we got a good idea of her "healthy" mental state. For example, when quizzed about her day, she stated that she had been to Sunday School and had eaten a good supper. In fact, both of these statements, while real in her mind, were false.

Mother was not back to normal.

Mother seemed to reach a plateau in her health after several weeks, although she began to have panic attacks. I had been on a walk and returned home to three voice messages. The social director and other staff had called repeatedly trying to reach me. Mother was lost and scared, but a few sentences from me on the phone and she was okay. Mother's phone calls to me increased in frequency, with no real purpose. She just needed to hear a familiar voice and then she could go on her way. The calls seemed to provide her the assurance she needed.

While Mother was on another plateau, unusual things still occurred: She again forgot the monthly devotion led by the pastor of our church, who she knew well and liked. I came over, saw the group was still meeting for their devotion, and encouraged her to attend, which she did. The pastor came by her apartment afterwards and began talking, as pastors are apt to do.

After 10 minutes or so, Mother got up from her chair and said as she approached the pastor, "I do not know who you are."

As Mother changed, I began to realize that I was changing too. I knew I was always on call. Every time I opened her apartment door, I feared what I would find. She began to call the house three or four times a day just to hear my voice. This often happened just after the extra help had left for the day, and I began to dread hearing the phone ring.

I had to remind myself that she suffered with dementia. If I reverted back to thinking about who she used to be, I would get angry at her comments and silly behavior. Why would she do that? Why would she say that? Why can't she remember that? She was not the Mother of years ago, or one year ago, or even of six months ago.

Part of my new awareness was that I soon found out that nothing she said was trustworthy. Certainly, her statements were not meant to be a lie (my Mother would *never* lie), but what she said reflected the way things used to be, or the way she remembered things, or maybe the way they should be. This idea went back to "willing it to be true." I knew this. I *wanted* to believe her; after all, she was my mother. But if I let down my guard and took her word for something, I was likely to get the wrong information. I did not want to miss how much food she was eating, how many laxatives she took, and what she had done that day: Had she actually done it? Did she only think she had done it? Should she have done it?

Further Decline; Further Confusion

The phone call was earlier than usual. Saturday morning was "Mother duty," and our extra help did not come in on weekends. But the call was early, about 7:30.

My mother began with a question: "Where's Mother?"

I paused for a bit. Then I questioned her to try and get up to speed on this first-of-a-kind question. I finally said that her mother had been dead for many years. Surprisingly, she was not disturbed but took the news in stride.

"So, Mother was not with me last night?" she asked.

I said no but then, to soften the situation, asked if she felt as though her mother was there. She then added, "So, Mother is not having her 91st birthday?"

She had put things together but just got the wrong person. My mother was turning 91 in January.

She quickly recovered to say, "So, I am the one with a birthday and not Mother. I guess you think I am just crazy."

I made it over to her apartment an hour later, and following breakfast and after some time had passed between us, I asked her if her mother had been in bed with her last night.

"It sure felt like it," she said. "I had crazy dreams all night long, but I was not frightened and they did not upset me."

Mother reached far back this time, pulling her own mother in close.

Mother Was Ever So Convincing

The next day, Sunday, was better. I went to Mother's apartment in the evening, and we had a relaxed talk about her impending move to Personal Care, which she was anticipating just a bit anxiously but overall looking forward to it.

Mother said she had had a good day and had gone to Sunday School at the retirement center. This statement caught my attention because I knew she had not gone to Sunday School in four months. So, I asked again, and again Mother answered that she had gone to Sunday School that day. I realized later that I should have asked what she studied. I left convinced that Mother had gone to Sunday School that day for the first time in a while. She was better and doing okay, it seemed.

In the library on the way out, however, I ran into a neighbor.

"How's your mother today?" the neighbor asked.

"Better," I replied.

Then she continued, "If you like, I would be pleased to pick her up on Sundays and walk her to Sunday School and then take her back. She was such a solid member."

I thanked her and then asked, "Didn't she come to Sunday School today?"

"Oh no," the neighbor quickly replied. "She hasn't been in weeks.

"I Know, But I Do Not Act"

As Mother's disease progressed and affected her memory, her decision-making ability diminished. She said more than once that she could not think, or think deeply, about situations. In her most sincere moments I heard her say, "Help me, Jesus, help me to think. I cannot think deeply."

Unlike before, thinking that required Mother to act was becoming impaired. In her better days, a water shutoff at the retirement center would have meant preparation, and Mother would have filled several gallon jugs with water just in case. But this time when I noticed there was no running water, Mother said, "Oh yes, there was an announcement the water would be off today."

The difference in how she reacted was that now there was no preparation. She knew the water was to be shut off, but she did nothing about it—including letting someone know. She had knowledge but did not, or could not, act.

I noticed Mother did this with other situations, and I thought she was in a new phase of her disease. She could not throw out old clothes she did not need. Sometimes Mother did not know, and other times she did know but did not act. The result of both situations was the same: nothing got done. I knew I had to be more aware for her.

I feared a worsening of her disease and that more would be required of me. I was not sure of what to do. Like Mother, I thought: "Jesus, help me; help me to think; help me to think deeply."

Personal Care Looming

Confusion and forgetfulness were pretty much a way of life now. Mother had moved beyond the initial shock of memory loss and confusion brought on by a low blood sodium level—blank stares and the continual questions of "What happened to me? Do you know what happened to me? Does everybody know what happened to me?" But she was at a plateau, much as the doctors had predicted. Some days were bright days when conversation was entertaining, and some days were dull when Mother focused on "her sickness." Predictably, as often happens with families dealing with this illness, during the bright days we reconsidered our decision and wondered if Mother really needed the next move. This attitude is called *denial* by the experts. But recalling that she forgot the preacher she knew well, how to turn off the television, and her way home from dinner reaffirmed the decision for the next move. Sadly, Mother had lost the ability to be independent and to care for herself.

Personal Care provided extra care and help, but Mother could still go outside on her own for walks. (This proved to be a real problem later on.) She seemed to be the ideal candidate for Personal Care. Our extra help was very good and gave Mother the care and companionship she needed, and I continued to go over daily and help out in the evenings. Luckily, Mother could stay by herself during the night, so I was able to leave about bedtime. We were hanging on … but anxiously wishing for Personal Care.

I thought back to the time when Mother first left her home to go to independent living. She was ready, even suggesting it. I was not so sure she was as ready for this next move. Mother never opposed the move to Personal Care and was generally positive, but it was not clear how much she understood, and at times she became confused. As she was apt to do, she began going to Personal Care to "look around." She talked to residents there, played extra games, and familiarized herself with the area. Pretty soon, she knew Personal Care better than she thought she did. Mother was pro-active about this move. She was deciding.

I developed a litany for Mother, repeating over and over again: "In Personal Care you will have more folks around and just more care. You will have three cooked meals a day, laundry service, help with medicines, and cleaning of your room." I must admit that I felt progress when Mother told one of my brothers that Personal Care would cook three meals a day and give her more care.

Mother also showed her old-time spunk at times as she thought about her next move. She would say that she had to be more active, clean her apartment, do things. She knew she was slipping from her work ethic and tidiness, and she desired to get back. But, she never could and she never did. The sad part was that she wanted to … sort of. She really enjoyed the help and pretty much doing nothing, but in her mind, she was doing many of the things she used to do. She would say as a matter of routine that she had been to the grocery store because it was Wednesday—senior day—and to Sunday School because it was Sunday. But she didn't go. I was not sure if she actually believed she had gone that day or if she was just remembering what used to be her routine. There might have been validity to the first idea, just as she honestly believed that people had stayed with her at night.

Preparing for Personal Care

The news came that a room would be available and we could prepare to move Mother. Her new apartment had two rooms and a large bathroom. I had wanted to keep this arrangement a surprise because when we first discussed the move, she seemed disappointed that she would leave a large apartment in independent living for just one room in Personal Care. The new living quarters were smaller than the current one, but there two rooms—a little mini-apartment.

"They have apartments with two rooms," she had said, indicating such a place would take some off the edge of "living down" to Personal Care. I was surprised that she knew about the two-room apartments. I wondered if she thought she needed more room or if the two-room apartment made her situation a little special. I also wondered about how much she really knew about Personal Care.

Mother was full of surprises. She had blasted one of my brothers with her demand of, "When are you boys going to take care of my move?" We both remembered the first move when her question then was, "When are you going to put a sign out front of the house?" We had already done all we could at this stage, and we were just waiting for the room to be renovated. The good news was that in her own way she had made herself ready, definitely and impatiently ready, to make this move to Personal Care. What another godsend!

Frantic Phone Calls

Despite making plans and constantly relating these plans to Mother, there was still more to deal with than before the move. Her phone calls to me increased during the day and early evening, and many calls, particular those in the evening, were often frantic. I could not identify any apparent incident that set her off, but there was always Mother's feeling of being "lost," accompanied by her forgetting how to turn off the television or to find something or someone. One time she requested: "I just realized last night that I need someone to take care of me. You need to find a place for me." We all noticed how far Mother had declined so quickly.

My wife and I had planned a three-week overseas trip. The last several days before our trip had been loaded with phone calls from Mother, some to just "touch bases" and some frantic. I suspected our impending travel was weighing heavily on her mind, although she denied it, and I wondered how much of the anxiety was caused by her impending move. I finally confronted her:

"Mother," I said, "is there anything that is making you anxious?"

"No, I am doing okay," she responded.

This was classic Mother "willing it to be."

Trying to get to the heart of the problem, one of which was the incessant, frantic phone calls, I mentioned that I feared she may have some anxieties over my travel and her move. She again replied that she was doing okay, and, contrary to my point, indicated that she thought she had handled everything very well

"Don't you think so?" she asked

I knew I could not just permit, but I had to *agree*.

"I have done okay since your Dad died, and I lived in that big old house alone and then moved here," Mother went on. "It has been hard, but I did okay. You just have to live," she said, summarizing the situation with her favorite axiom.

She then moved into "pontification mode" in which she posited an ideal view of living. After a while, I stopped her and said, "I am not interested in how everyone else lives; I am interested in you. Are you okay?"

"Yes, it's been hard, but I am doing okay. Don't you think so?"

I chose the "it's been hard" part to explore.

"I know it has been hard, but what specifically makes you call it hard?"

"Well," she began slowly, "you know about half my family is gone now."

Yes, all of her siblings and her father and mother had passed away. But I wondered where this was going, so I questioned more.

"You know," she continued, "everyone moved away, and there is not the closeness. Of course, that is life and I would not try to bring them all back together."

It was not clear if Mother was talking about her siblings or her own children. Indeed, we had all moved away after college and marriage. I asked if she was upset when, after a break, her brothers and sisters went back to college.

"I cried for a week," she blurted out. "It would always upset me so when they left. Separations have always been so hard for me. Change has been hard for me."

I picked up the discussion of separation within her growing-up family again, the family that had since passed away. She talked for some time about these times. Mother was the only one of her family who did not go off to college. She was home until she married, and even then she lived near her parents. Her first two sons were born in her parents' family home.

I knew she and my grandmother were close, and she thought her mother was ideal. I got a further glimpse into Mother's view of her family, closeness, separation, and loneliness she felt so intensely. I remembered all those people who "stayed with her at night" and slept in her bed. They were usually family members—most often sisters.

Still (Futilely) Trying to Work Out This Illness

I will confess to frustration. I was home from running errands long before Mother's first phone call that morning. She was just "touching bases." Soon, the second call came, and she was crying: "I am lost. I can't find my clothes to get dressed. Can you come over?"

When I arrived 30 minutes later, Mother was getting dressed and doing okay. She was still a bit anxious, but that did not keep me from being upset with her. She told me not to lecture her. She knew I was upset at having to come over. Although she was functioning, getting ready and doing everything like always, was it possible that a panic attack was happening? I wanted to find out. I did not apologize for lecturing her but tried to put a positive spin on my statements.

"You are in a different time of life now," I began, "and you will want to do some of the things you can do personally. You do not need to rush or become anxious. If you feel such a feeling coming over you, just sit down and let it pass."

She nodded in agreement and apologized again for being a bother.

"I never wanted it to come to this and to be a bother to my children," she said tearfully.

I still was not ready to let go of this new approach, so I continued: "We need to find another way to deal with the anxiety. Look at you now, just thirty minutes after you called me. You are dressed and ready to go. If you could just realize that the anxiety will pass in a few minutes."

My hope was that she would learn to deal with panic attacks. However, while I was on my walk, Mother called five times in 45 minutes. She was frantic. This time the staff had taken her to visit Personal Care. When I arrived, she *ran* to me like a little lost girl and hugged me.

I first hoped that a harsh strategy of "just do it" would work. It did not. Then I tried a strategy of honesty. I told Mother that things would not get better, she would not go back to keeping house, or taking medicines alone, or handling her affairs. I was desperate for a way forward.

I knew so little of the disease and how to deal with Mother or myself. I told her: "This is where we are in life. It will not get better. It is not your fault; it is just where we are in life now. We are thankful we have a good home, money to pay bills, and people to care for us for the rest of our lives."

She thanked me for telling her this truth and said she would work with everyone. She used the word "crazy" several times, but I used the word "confused." I never used the words crazy, or Alzheimer's. Later, she realized she dreamed up things, and people she thought were present were not. Mother said her mind was weak. I agreed, but repeated that it was not her fault, that this was where we were now in life. Mother was trying to deal with her confusion, trying to be in control of the uncontrollable. It was not her fault. But neither could she do anything about it.

One Monday, Mother called twice and wanted me to come over. I first saw the Personal Care director but got no word on when the room renovation would start or finish. I then went to Mother's apartment. She was confused. She had taken her pocketbook to a music program in the library and lost her billfold and coin purse. I found them in the office, where they had been turned in by someone. Mother kept repeating that she had "messed up" and "messed everyone up." Mother hated to mess up. She was always focused on doing everything just right and in knowing her status—her internal, controlled order.

At this point, and after another episode of the lost pocketbook, Mother and I had a long talk about her problems and her "anxiety." We now had a word to describe her condition. Over the next four or five days, Mother had many anxiety attacks, including confusion and a pounding chest. She could not remember what happened and would not quit calling me and wanting me to go over. I wondered if the medicine Namenda prescribed by the neurologist made her confusion worse. As the dosage increased, Mother showed heightened anxiety about two to three hours after the morning dose.

Honesty and Sensitivity

My times with Mother were not without flare-ups, as indicated by a discussion after a routine doctor's visit. Everything physical about Mother—her weight, blood pressure, and so on—was about as good as could be expected for an approaching 91-year-old.

On the return home, more than once she asked, "How am I?"

"Fine," I replied. "Everything is fine."

"Did the doctor say that?"

"Yes," I said, "she said you were fine."

"How do you think I am?" she continued.

While I accepted the doctor's conclusion, Mother needed additional assurance. Now, I thought, is a time for honesty with sensitivity.

"I think you focus too much on yourself," I said, not realizing the wide, wide door I had just opened.

"You do? You think I am talking about myself too much?" she asked incredulously.

I tried to hold my ground. I repeated that I did indeed think she focused on herself too much, and, trying to take the edge off a bit, added that it was not good for her. I suggested she talk about other subjects such as old Christmases and when she and Dad had the jewelry store. We did … for just a moment. And then she went back to talking about herself again. Mother was appalled that she had done this and promised to mend her ways. She promised … and then she asked again if she talked too much about herself.

Continuing with the theme of honesty and sensitivity, I said, "You are doing it again. You are talking about yourself."

The honesty was there, but my sensitivity was a bit light.

"Just stop and let it go. We have gone over this ground, and nothing more needs to be said!" I was flustered and maybe even mad. Mother would not let go of her astonishment that she was talking about herself continually.

Back in her apartment, after I said some words in anger, Mother insisted, "You have to let me say this."

I certainly could not prevent her from talking about herself, but now I was fed up and responded with, "Do not tell me what to do! Do *not* tell me what to do!"

That pretty much ended the conversation. Of course, I had regrets over my flare-up. Did I go too far? Was I too heavy on the honest and too light on the sensitive? I concluded I was not.

A day or so later, Mother mentioned that she felt defeated and discouraged. Yes, she was talking about herself again, but in a different way.

On another day, she woke up agitated. She had not slept well that night and was cranky the next morning. Mother was frustrated by her condition, the stiffness in her legs, and the nagging cough. We had our second confrontation in just a few days.

"I wish I had a real doctor that I could go to, like I used to," Mother said with agitation.

"What do you think your doctor now is?" I asked, equally agitated.

"Is she a doctor?" Mother continued.

"Yes," I said. "Why do you think you have been seeing her for seven years?"

Very soon Mother showed contriteness and even apologized for being like she was. When a brother called later, she said that she had been ornery that morning, and laughed. I got on the phone and said *I* had been ornery too, and she laughed again. We had made up.

The Dead Past; the Unborn Future

A few days before Mother moved to Personal Care, I thought it would be good to clear out some items, particularly clothes and shoes, that Mother did not wear and pocketbooks that she did not use. At first, she resisted. Perhaps the impending move was building up emotions, or perhaps it was the clothes themselves that evoked her feelings. Either way, she was unable to give up any clothes or shoes or pocketbooks.

"I just can't think about that now," she said.

Being practical, I did not know where everything would go, but I also realized we could take this conversation no further.

It was like the preacher had said on Sunday, "… being between a dead past and the unborn future." Although the preacher was talking about something else, I thought of Mother. Her move to independent living was done with a lot of hope. The move to Personal Care did not carry as much of that hope.

Mother knew for sure she was moving, but she just could not put all the facts together. "Where is my new room?" she would ask many times a day. "Will I live here until I move? What will I do with my things I cannot take along?" I could see the wheels trying—but failing—to turn. Mother sat and pondered often. Despite all my attempts to comfort and persuade her of good things, there still was an unborn future ahead of us.

Notes

[1] Tom Brokaw, *The Greatest Generation* (Random House, New York, 1998).

[2] Maud Richman Calvert, *Every Day Living for Boys and Girls* (Richmond, VA: Smith, Hammond & Co., 1929).

[3] Katheryn P. Darr, in *Journey Through the Bible*, vol. 8, "Ezekiel" (Nashville: Abingdon Press, 2000), 44.

Chapter 2
Personal Care

Adjusting Again

At first, Mother seemed to adjust very well to her new surroundings and new friends. Her apartment was just across the hall from the dining room, which doubled as the bingo parlor. She enjoyed having everything close by, as she had become less interested in long walks to the dining room or other places. Everything was "cozy," that being her word, so, we left her in her new digs.

The happiness, however, did not last long, and two days later at noon I received a frantic call.

"I need you to come over, NOW! I need you to check on me. I need you to come NOW!"

I asked what was wrong, hoping we could handle this situation over the phone.

"I need you to come over, NOW," she repeated.

Mother was overwrought, and then I became overwrought, telling her that I could not "come over" there every time she wanted me to. I had things to do.

Mother threw down the gauntlet.

"Come over and check on me, *or I will die!*" she said and hung up.

I did, therefore, go over there. I found her seated at the dining table, alone, and waiting … for what, I didn't know. She seemed a bit surprised to see me but happy nonetheless. As I suspected, nothing was really wrong; she just needed to know where she was—reassurance that could come only, it seemed, by my presence or that of a family member. I tried to be firm about coming over, and we made it through this situation still friends.

The second tension-filled moment came because of a bathroom fixture in her new apartment: a toilet that was raised on a two-inch pedestal.

Despite evidence to the contrary, Mother was emphatic that she could not use the toilet and hadn't been in two days. I pointed out that we had given the "pedestal potty" a trial run before we moved in and agreed it would work. She denied that we had done this, and when I explained to her that management said the toilet could not be lowered, she replied "I don't believe a word of it."

Staff placed a temporary, portable toilet next to the "pedestal potty," which Mother mostly ignored. I would visit every other day, and Mother seemed happy, although still confused at times as to where things were. On every visit she would want to show me her new living room, closet, and bathroom—and sometimes the temporary toilet. We quit speaking of the problem of the "pedestal potty," and I noticed on a later visit that the portable toilet was missing from the bathroom.

Mother Is Beginning to Forget Us

I continued the Sunday afternoon visits. This was habit for me and a time without activities for Mother. Her 91st birthday was approaching fast. We talked of several things, including Sunday naps—probably because I woke her from hers when I arrived. I reminisced to her about how Dad would go the extra step in the usual Sunday afternoon nap. With his tedious job repairing watches and trying to make a living in a small town, Dad worked hard and long hours. He deserved a Sunday afternoon nap, and often he crawled into bed rather than settling for just a chair before visiting his own mother.

Then Mother said, "I do not think of your dad so often anymore."

Her memory of Dad seemed to be fading. This statement made me sad. She and Dad had a good, maybe even great, marriage. Dad was Mother's first love, the one you do not ever forget. They truly loved each other, made it through spats and disputes, earned a living so three boys could go to college and so Mother could live to be at least 91 on their savings. Yes, they had a great marriage. Now, though, her memory of Dad was fading. Mother was forgetting him.

But what was still vividly clear to Mother was her growing-up family, especially her siblings.

"I dreamed Audie was in bed with me last night," Mother said. "I have thought of Audie a lot lately. You know that Aubrie and Audie [twins four years older than Mother] would have a birthday on January 23."

I admit I was surprised at her comment. The day Mother had moved into her new apartment was my birthday, and she did not mention it at all. She did not mention it this day either; nor did she remember my brothers' birthdays. Our birthdays were lost to her. While we were not particularly hurt by this omission, we noticed what seemed to fade away and what seemed to remain in Mother's memory.

The road of dementia is not consistent among sufferers, I was told, and family members could not know what to expect. Mother's oldest sister, Aunt Lilly, was 12 years older than Mother. Before she died at age 98, Aunt Lilly had dementia and probably Alzheimer's disease. I thought back to the last visits Mother and I had with Aunt Lilly in the nursing home some 10 years earlier. Mother would sit and talk to Aunt Lilly, telling her about her husband and their three sons. Aunt Lilly would listen attentively but then retain none of what was said about her family. It was strikingly sad in my mind that Aunt Lilly had lost the memory of her beloved family.

How much had *we* faded away? I wondered. I began to prepare for the time when I would walk in and Mother would not know me. That had not happened yet ... but it would.

"My Mother Could Do Everything"

The Sunday afternoon visits continued for Mother and me in her new Personal Care apartment. They were sometimes enjoyable, but not always, and the conversation became stale—stuck on health, the weather, and her new apartment. I embarked on a new strategy. I wanted to know more details about Mother's life growing up, things I regretted never having discussed with her before: What was so memorable to her about her upbringing and her family? What did she feel about her brothers and sisters? What did she feel about her mother and dad? A good way to get into such conversations, I found, was a common denominator with Mother, Grandmother, and me: gardening.

"How did Grandmother get her plants for her garden?" I began.

That's all it took for Mother to strike out down memory lane. In rapid succession came stories on the vegetable garden, canning, the wood stove, and the new pressure cooker Granddad bought for Grandmother.

"My mother could do everything," Mother said. "She raised her own plants from seed and had a big garden every year."

During this discussion about Grandmother, I discovered several things. One was practical information on how to grow sweet potatoes, but a more important one was how Mother felt about her mother. I think "adored" would be the word to use.

"My mother could do everything," she repeated.

"How did she learn to do all these things?" I asked.

"She attended home demonstration clubs led by Mrs. Whatley," Mother replied.

Mother amazed me that day with the details, even recalling the instructor's name. (I confess that I wondered if she really got the name right.)

"Mrs. Whatley taught canning and all sorts of things. Mother would can in jars and in cans."

On one Sunday afternoon visit shortly after some of our talks on family, a brother brought an article he had recently found about Mother's home area. Reading through the old pages typed out by the local amateur historian inspired Mother even more, perhaps jogging her memory of things she had not thought about in a long time. Amazingly, she and the article agreed on almost everything. The article even verified the name of Mrs. Whatley, the home demonstration agent who led clubs on canning.

Three Worlds

The first two months of Personal Care were a time of adjustment, with agitation alternating with calmness. On a Wednesday afternoon visit I found Mother sitting in her easy chair with a smile on her face; she seemed at ease and at home.

"This is a good place for me," she said.

We walked outside the building, Mother using her walker. She commented on the beautiful spring day, with warm sunshine and a temperature in the upper 70s. We saw the new Memory Care unit adjacent to Personal Care, which was being finished, then went back and walked a little more in the hallways. Her walk was slow and measured, as she talked and commented on various things.

As we walked past two occupied rooms, I asked, "Are they your tablemates?"

"Yes, they are."

I was pleased that she recognized their names on the doors, even though she could not come up with them from scratch.

Earlier, Mother had said she felt that her sister Audie had been with her a lot lately.

"It seems so real, Audie here with me and helping me," she said.

When I asked Mother about Audie's helping her, Mother stated that Aubrie (or A.B. as she often called her brother) was doing some things and that Audie was in the background. I am not sure who was "present" mostly, but Audie and Aubrie the twins seemed to be in her mind.

At this time Mother seemed to exist in three worlds: The first world was with Audie and her siblings and other "visitors from the family," a situation that was not distressing but was, in fact, comforting to Mother. Then there was the world in which real family visited, mostly my brothers and me and occasionally a grandchild or niece. Mother always enjoyed these visits, seemed to rally from them, and fretted a lot when we left. Mother once summed up her hope: "I wish we all lived together in one big house," she said.

World three was her daily life without real or imaginary family. This world included the staff, her tablemates, bingo buddies, and those who sat and slept in the sitting room. I did not know much about this world, and she did not talk much about it. Although she inhabited this world, recalling names, events, or situations often seemed beyond her. She lived in this world very well and comfortably, but Mother described it to us only in the broadest outline. As I later discovered, however, she was more active in this world than I knew.

Some Calmness

Three months into Personal Care, Mother had adjusted to her new apartment, and her phone calls were less frequent. I also noticed her calmness and pleasant expression as we sat and talked on Sundays. Despite her inability to remember recent events, Mother began to worry less. She was getting into a routine and getting to "know the ropes." Further, there were socials and exercise classes. Of course, having three hot meals a day prepared, room cleaning, laundry service, and folks always around to give you medicine and remind you of events could be easy to get used to. This was the first time in Mother's life that so much was being done *for* her.

Even with loss of memory, Mother found a way to continue to live with grace and honor, and to remain pretty much in character. There were times when she was confused and could not remember, but she was happier and seemed resigned to her age and limitations.

For sure there were days without calmness, such as when she called before 8 a.m. and apologetically asked if I knew about her hair wash. I told her that staff there would give her a bath and wash her hair that morning. I went over later to see how things were, and we talked. First, I had to assure her that I was okay; then, I had to assure her that she was okay. This took the form of reassuring her she was in the right place, that she was doing fine, that she was acting herself and behaving, and that money was okay. Unlike past times, she had no confidence in her judgment.

After two weeks of infrequent calls, Mother began calling again. She seemed concerned but could not state the problem. She called once to say she was not getting her medicine, and although she knew she should take medicine, she could not remember when she did. The same happened with doctors' appointments. Often, Mother would have in the back of her mind the notion that she should be going somewhere, but she could not remember when or where. Not knowing the whens and wheres bothered her. She knew she believed the Bible and the stories in it, but she could not remember what they were. So, even though Mother's life still reflected who she was and her character, it was different now because she could not remember details.

Going into the fourth month after the move to Personal Care, Mother began to complain again about being lonely. She attached herself closely to me through very frequent, phone calls. One day she called five times, with three in the evening, and the last just after 9 p.m. While she started the last conversation with an upbeat, "How are ya tonight?" it was easy to tell that her mind was foggy. Finally, after a few moments of chitchat, she asked, "Where am I?"

It seemed that the disease had progressed, and Mother could not sort out where she was, how she got there, and how things such as expenses and money worked. She would say, "Since I am away from my home …," implying that she was recently, and maybe temporarily, away from her home. Although she had resided in independent living for almost eight years, Mother seemed not to remember that time at all. She often commented, "If I don't think about things, they are far back in my mind."

Mother and I Go to the Dentist—Again

After birthday number 91, Mother and I had our semi-annual dentist visits. This was for routine cleanings, but often Mother had a cavity or two. I had not succeeded in getting her to try an electric toothbrush, which I thought would give her better cleaning, and I did not know how well her teeth were brushed. Dentist visits were always a worry about new cavities.

We started this adventure about 10:30 a.m. Luckily, "Big Breakfast," the once-a-month dining extravaganza that everyone looked forward to, had been postponed until the following week, giving us more time—a good omen for the day. Mother was dressed when I arrived and had told the staff that she was going to the dentist that morning. As we prepared to leave, I noticed that Mother had her pocketbook out and ready to go. I tried to persuade her for practical reasons to leave it in her apartment whenever we went somewhere; she did not have any money or identification in it and continually worried about where it was. I was afraid I would forget she brought it with her.

"I feel lost without my pocketbook," she argued slightly.

"You do not need it," I responded.

"I always like to have my pocketbook with me," she continued.

"You do not need it," I repeated.

Finally, she agreed not to take the pocketbook and put it back in the drawer.

As we were leaving, she asked "Now what did I do with my pocketbook?"

Our subsequent conversation driving over to the dentist's office most likely related to the pocketbook, as I later realized.

"Now, how will we pay for this visit?" Mother asked.

"I will put in on my credit card," I said, "and settle up with you later."

"You be sure and get your money," she reiterated to me as she had done on many previous occasions. Interestingly, our discussion over money was not the usual one that people have. It was not concerned with "do you owe *me* money?" but rather "do I owe *you* money?" Mother was very concerned that I would get reimbursed. Mother and Dad had always wanted to pay off their debts as soon as possible, and Mother still felt that way.

As we drove on, Mother started again, "How do I pay for these things?"

I responded rather sharply: "Mother! I am taking care of you. You have sufficient money, and I will look after your accounts. Whenever these thoughts come into mind about your money and how you pay for things, try to remember that I am taking care of them. You do not need to worry."

Mother quietly responded, "Well, I am not worrying. It's just in my position now. You need something to talk about, and I am just *talking* about this."

We both laughed and continued on to the dentist.

Mother had another cavity. The dentist had no time that day to do a filling, so we made an appointment to return the following day at 5 p.m. As we were leaving, I told Mother we had to return to fix her cavity.

"They didn't tell me I had a cavity," she said a bit indignantly.

"Maybe you didn't hear them."

"She did not tell me," Mother repeated.

"Maybe the hygienist didn't know and the dentist is the one who found it," I said.

"No, she knew and did not tell me."

I could not think how to, or if I should, continue this line of discussion.

"He could have just filled it today," Mother said, showing *she* could continue.

"He has other patients and did not have an appointment available today."

"It would not have taken long," Mother said.

"But how would you feel if someone took *your* appointment," I hopefully concluded.

She agreed that it would not be fair. I do not think we necessarily settled this discussion, but it drifted away.

The Tea Party

The retirement home hosted its first-ever tea party on the eve of Mother's Day in Mother's 91st year. The day was bright and sunny, and my older brother and his wife came to visit. Appropriately, the party included tea—a peach-apricot fruity tea that was very tasty. Place settings with matching plates and tea cups of various designs were on the tables. The dining room was full of folks from both Independent Living and Personal Care. We had a few announcements, some thank yous, a light lunch, music, and a guest speaker.

All went well until the latter part of the event. Mother's demeanor was unusual; she seemed away in her own little world. As the speaker wore on, Mother became more and more annoyed. I was annoyed too, so I understood why Mother looked at her watch several times. While Mother glared at the speaker, she refrained from any comments until we were in her apartment.

There she spoke, "It was a disaster!"

While "inappropriate," "vulgar," and "too much about me" certainly described much of the speech, we all wondered exactly why Mother summarized it as "a disaster." It turns out that it had to do with holding folks down for a long time, maybe even "against their will." I agreed because I wanted to leave but could not find a way to do it; I, too, felt held against my will.

"We are not used to sitting still for so long," Mother stated.

I agreed, again. However, my unproven opinion is that Mother actually heard more than we thought she did. She heard the speaker make fun of her mother choosing a gaudy casket, telling of her mother's constant scolding, and the vulgar language. As the afternoon wore on in Mother's apartment and the tea party was exhaustively analyzed, Mother continued to express less than praise for the latter portion of the program. With some prodding, however, she acknowledged that the food was good. From that experience I learned to never underestimate what Mother heard!

Memory Care Looming?

As we moved into the fifth month of Personal Care, some days were good and some were just okay. Mother often greeted me with: "My mind is foggy today. I just cannot remember." And I heard less frequently, "But I am getting better."

It was not clear what Mother thought about her future. I had avoided talking about Alzheimer's disease and wondered if she suspected she suffered from this illness or from some form of dementia. She never mentioned it. Hesitatingly, I broached the opening of the new Memory Care unit at her retirement center. The official name is the Center for Alzheimer's and Dementia Care.

Mother's wise response was: "It is good to have those places. So many people are living longer and need that care."

I agreed. She still never mentioned that she might have Alzheimer's, although she used to ask often what I thought was wrong with her. Since there is currently no definitive test to diagnose Alzheimer's in a living person, I did not lie by saying that I did not know what was wrong. (In fact, Mother did not show some signs readily associated with Alzheimer's, and up to the end I was not sure that it was the correct diagnosis.) I couched it by saying, "you have some memory loss," or, "you are confused at times."

I told Mother I was going to the open house of the new center that Sunday and asked if she would like to go. She said no to my offer twice, and I did not insist. I wondered if she was avoiding it. On Sunday, after a walk within the center, I went to her room. She was not there, but I saw her in the sitting room holding forth with another of the residents. She glanced up at me and then continued her conversation. At first, I thought she did not recognize me. So I moved closer and tried to hide behind the door to overhear her conversation.

"That's my son over there," I heard her say. "He came to visit me."

So, she did recognize me after all. I got the impression, however, that she would have just as soon continued her visit in the sitting room.

Mother and I chatted a while about the day, then she allowed that earlier she had gone over to see the center and it was very nice.

"It is good to have this place because so many people need this care," she repeated.

It was not important for her to know that she was on the waiting list.

I stayed only a few minutes that day. She did not seem to want to hold me there like she usually did, as she was having an excellent day and enjoying the interactions with other residents.

I pondered the new center and Mother. Would she need that extra care soon, or would she remain as she was for a while? As I thought about this circumstance, I overheard a friend in the hallway say to his mother, "No, Mother, I am not Edward. I am your son Harry." I felt sorry for him and his mother and wondered how long it would be before it was my turn to say that.

Mother Is Just Sorry

Mother would often say, "I am just sorry. I do not do anything anymore." Mother's use of the word "sorry" reminded me of a colleague from outside the South who had heard that a certain person was "just sorry." Having heard this particular expression applied more than once, my colleague finally asked what the person was sorry (meaning apologetic) about. It had to be explained that the person was not "apologetically" sorry but was "no-account" sorry. He did not do anything useful—he was just sorry.

Mother used the term "sorry" to wrap up her view of work, retirement, old age, and her disappointment at her inability to do what she used to do. I reflected on Mother's dilemma, remembering that I, too, having retired two years earlier was also concerned about becoming sorry. Perhaps it was the Protestant work ethic that was instilled in me. We boys were lucky to grow up in a little town where we could work in the summer and on weekends—and we did. From elementary school onward, we all worked as paper boys or in similar employment around school or football. This work ethic and work history shaped our lives and remained with us when we retired. I often thought about what I had accomplished, what useful thing I had done that day, or what intellectual thing I had pursued.

When Mother was having one of her "I am just sorry" moments, I laughingly asked, "Do you want to go and plow the back forty?" Laughingly she replied, "No, I will just have to live where I am. I am in a good place." Despite her dementia, Mother remembered her work ethic. While she knew the days of doing things were gone, she still seemed to miss being useful and accomplishing something. Neither Mother nor I wanted to be sorry. We were seeking the same thing.

Trauma and Drama Over the Permanent

Monday was a good day for Mother, as was Sunday. In fact, she seemed to be doing extraordinarily well. Then Tuesday arrived.

I received the first call at 8 a.m. concerning something Mother thought she had to do. "I just can't remember what I was to do. I need someone to help me work it out," she implored. I could tell she was really lost and likened it to a person released in a foreign city with no friends, no knowledge of where to go or what to do, no idea of where to find answers, and unable to speak the language.

"I need a permanent," she said. "What do you think?"

I replied, "A few weeks ago we discussed a permanent, and the hairdresser did not think you needed one."

"I don't care," she said firmly. "I need a permanent. I cannot do anything with my hair. The people here said I needed to have something done with my hair."

It was clear that Mother had no recollection of the beauty salon in her complex or any knowledge of who did hair there. I suggested Mother talk to the staff and ask them to help her set up an appointment, but she kept asking if she should go to the office. Finally, Mother said she would ask the staff in her hallway and let me know. She called back a few minutes later to tell me they would set up an appointment for her to get a permanent.

But then Mother got confused as to how she would get to the beauty shop. I reminded her that the staff would take her. She said she needed to go back to the office and make sure. She then called me again to say the appointment was set up for Thursday. This was surprising because I thought the beautician was there only on Wednesdays. But surely the staff knew better than I. My job was to come over and pay, which I said I would do. Mother seemed relieved that this big ordeal was over.

Unfortunately, the next day was no better, and possibly worse. Mother called me at 7:20 a.m.—the earliest she had ever called. I knew she was totally confused about what to do. She was looking for some answers, for some relief from the doubt.

"Can you tell me what I am supposed to do? Do I have an appointment for a permanent today? I cannot get any information from the workers here," she railed on.

"You told me it was Thursday," I replied. "Is that right?"

"I don't know. I am just so confused, and I cannot get anyone to tell me."

Mother was not in tears, but near, I thought. We discussed her going to the staff and finding out when the appointment was. She seemed relieved that there was a plan, although not yet an answer. She then called again and asked me much the same question but from the staff desk. They had told her they were too busy at that time to tend to the matter. My guess was that she had worn them out with incessant requests on the permanent. I asked to speak to someone.

A staff member came on the phone and said they had not yet made an appointment but would do so as soon as the beauty salon opened. Mother got back on the phone, and I explained the plan to her. I asked her not to ask the staff anymore but to give them time to check with the beauty shop. She agreed, but then she called back a little later. She still could not keep the plan straight. I asked her again not to go back to the staff but to let them set up an appointment. I knew I needed to make a trip over there as soon a possible.

I visited at noon, made an excuse for coffee in the dining room, and checked with the staff. The beautician had not shown up that day, but the staff person said she would see to an appointment the next day. I thanked her. She said she thought Mother had settled down a bit, and I was sure they were tired of seeing her. With my presence and a plan, Mother at last seemed to be relaxing.

As we talked, she said she was not concerned about a permanent and it could wait a while. That was not what I'd been hearing for two days! Why the sudden calmness? I am not sure, other than the fact that someone else was in charge and making decisions. I counted seven phone calls over two days about this permanent. Regardless of how she parsed it now, it *was* a big deal.

Milk of Magnesia

Milk of Magnesia and the need for it resurfaced many times during Mother's stay in both Independent Living and Personal Care. It caused more tension and anger than any other thing. Early on, the doctor had told us that we should get Mother off laxatives, and we three sons had made a heroic effort.

If there was ever a woman who could beat you down on a topic, it was Mother. We suggested she eat apples, bran, more apples, more bran, and most everything natural. But Mother trusted Milk of Magnesia. She knew it acted quickly, and she was well-versed in laxative-taking. There were times we were willing to give her the laxative to have some relief ourselves.

I found it impossible to keep this delicate but difficult issue to myself. As I mentioned Mother's problem to others, I discovered that bathroom behavior of this nature was very common among older women (and men?)—and apparently not just with ones living with dementia.

Over the years, we revisited the subject repeatedly.

"Would you bring me some Milk of Magnesia?" Mother would ask. "Just when you go to the store."

"I cannot bring that to you," I would tell her. "The staff has to give it to you."

Rules did not allow family members to medicate residents.

Mother was already being given Metamucil every day, but in the interest of maintaining our sanity, the doctor agreed to send a note to the staff allowing them to give Mother some Milk of Magnesia on occasion, should she ask for it. The plan worked for a long while, until we once again found ourselves at loggerheads.

On this day, Mother was begging for Milk of Magnesia, and I was stonewalling. Both of us were upset.

"I would do anything for you," she pleaded, "and you will not help me. If you are not going to bring me some Milk of Magnesia, then don't come!"

On a previous visit, a staff member told me that Mother had come to the staff station and they had given her a cup—a goodly amount—of Milk of Magnesia. I mulled this new information over as I went to her room for a visit.

"I never want to be a burden to my children," Mother said. "I know about old ladies and how they can be, and I do not want to be like that."

Most of the visit was spent in mild arguing, with Mother criticizing staff and getting confused between the Personal Care doctor and her own doctor (who she was scheduled to visit) and restating her need for Milk of Magnesia so she could empty her bowels. It was as though Mother was trapped in a mind and body that would not function as she thought it should—or as she remembered. Mother was lost, but she was also angry.

Finally, she volunteered: "I did go to the bathroom this morning."

My jaw dropped. "We have been discussing this issue all day, and now you tell me you did go to the bathroom?"

Mother's expression was one of surprise at what she had just said. She repeated her comment. Then, she expressed anger at herself for not knowing, for not being able to remember, for acting like the old ladies she knew. Back at home I pondered what had happened. It seemed our strategies for coping with this issue were no longer working. There was no hope for a better day. I feared we were moving toward another stage, and just getting through it might be the only way.

At one point, the head nurse weighed in. "Let me tell you something about women of this age," she said. "The situation is very common. I am dealing with it now with my grandparents. They think they have to go to the bathroom every day or there is a problem." The fact that Mother was *normal* was only slightly welcome news. As the social director had once said, the only thing "normal" was the setting on the washing machine.

Telephone Abuse

At the time I thought I was the only one, and only later did I discover that Mother was calling all three of her sons incessantly. Mother now seemed to live outside reality much of the time, and her only salvation was to call me. I was a point of reference, and I thought about how to proceed.

First, do no harm, I thought. It was not easy for me not to become frustrated with Mother's continued calls and questions on the same subject. Second, I tried to be as calming as I could while at the same time being honest. I tried to encourage her, but she could not remember where she was or why she was there. She would thank me for showing her kindness by letting her talk to me and said it made her feel better. Mother knew she was having problems.

Unfortunately, the phone calls increased to the point that I had to look for another strategy than just letting her call constantly. A pattern had emerged: Eat, walk, call. Eat, walk, call. Eat, walk, call. While I first thought my talking to her was a good thing, I began to doubt that it was. I became very tired of her calling so often, and I'm sure it showed. In trying to find another, better way, I broached the subject:

"Mother, you call and say you are lonesome," I began. "What do you really mean by that?"

"I just feel lonesome. Nobody is here but me, and since I left my home ..."

I interrupted her and said, "Mother, you have been away from your home for 10 years. Is that what is really wrong?"

She started again, "I'm okay. It is just that I am trying to get myself settled. I will do better."

I am sure she could feel tension in my voice. I tried to tone down the level to suggest my plan.

"Why don't you watch television? Find some programs and look forward to seeing them at night."

"I am not interested in television. There is nothing I want to see," Mother stated firmly.

I encouraged her to look at the baseball games, reminding her how much she used to enjoy watching them. But she was not interested in baseball, or religious programs, or game shows. At my insistence in trying to find some activity she would enjoy, she lost interest in my comments too.

"I don't like to have to explain myself all the time!" she said with a little anger.

I retorted, "If you are going to call me several times a day, I think I have the right to try to help you find a way to be happier."

During one of our not-too-pleasant discussions, Mother retreated with a promise to "never say she was lonesome again." This wasn't much of a plan. No one could blame her for trying to ward off the loneliness. I thought about saying something after her next visit to the neurologist, but since he told me *his* mother called him five times a day I had to assume there was no medical remedy, no sympathy, and, sadly, no way forward. Ideally, I hoped to get her into television-watching on a regular basis so she could come home and look forward to a familiar face and voice—one that was not mine.

There was no way to approach the phone-call issue without some hurt feelings.

"It is not the calling; it is just that I fear you are not happy, and I do not know what to do to help. You are in perfect health, no pains, and everything is taken care of. You have all sorts of folks helping you and a good, safe place to live. If we could just find a way to stop those lonely feelings when you come home at night, you would be better. I wish I knew how to help you."

Mother replied, "Well, I won't do that ever again. I don't know what causes those feelings. Do you?" The phone calls declined to one or two a day, usually in the morning and in the evening to talk to someone and "touch bases." It was like a check to know where she was and for me to know where she was, as though I might forget.

"I May Just Have to Move Back Home"

"Are you coming to see me today? I am so lonely," Mother began the phone conversation early on a Sunday afternoon. "I may just have to move back home." I was not sure if she meant her growing-up home or where we boys had grown up. What was most disturbing, though, was this was the first time since leaving her home 10 years earlier that Mother had mentioned going back.

My plan had been to fill the Sunday afternoon visits with talk about various things of Mother's interest and knowledge—religion, family, and gardening—but today I focused on the word "lonely." I really wanted to jump on her for saying she may have to move back home, but I thought better of it. But we did talk most of the time about being lonely. I told her I wanted to know more of how she felt, what she really meant by lonely, and what we could do to help the situation. We spent the time discussing Mother's feelings, the fact that she just got up and did what she needed to do, and "just lived." That is not the way I had been seeing it for the past few weeks. There seemed to be a constant fret about being lonely whenever she called. I am sure she was, but when she was engaged with activities such as bingo, she was not lonely. She was *engaged*.

The remarkable thing to me was Mother's ability to describe herself, without any real details. As we talked, I tried not to sound overbearing, and Mother tried to tell me her feelings. "I guess it is my time of life," she said, repeating a stock phrase she had learned. This idea took any responsibility or failure on her part away, and that was the problem I saw. Mother was not "just living," but constantly fretting about her situation. In a moment of insight, she added: "I guess I do not have any enthusiasm anymore. I used to do everything and stay busy and stay up on things. I do not do that anymore."

In truth, she probably did not have the interest to stay enthused or the ability to really dig into things anymore. Even though there were enough things available to keep her busy, she didn't have any enthusiasm. I then did a very "man" thing, trying to solve the problem for her instead of just listening. I kept interrupting her self-diagnosis with suggestions. "Maybe you could get involved with some television programs, like baseball, that you used to enjoy and look forward to," I offered (again).

I did not get much of a response when I mentioned calling her sons when she wanted to talk with them. She said only, "I have never been one to talk much on the phone. I do not have much to say. I will just let them call me when they want to talk." I raised my eyebrows. I did not get much of a response either when I suggested more reading materials. She had *plenty* to read.

As I think back on our transition, both Mother's and mine, I realize how inadequate my comments and approach were. I was asking Mother to identify her problem and to find a solution. She could not do either. My dilemma continued because I still did not know much about the disease or how to deal with it. At times, Mother would get personal and a little defiant. "When you get old, you will see what I mean," she said.

Mother was giving me all the answers she could. She was also showing me the new normal in her life now. She had done all that she could do. She had been responsible.

After a lengthy, and I am sure, frustrating conversation for her, Mother asked me if I understood better now. I responded that I did. I was sincere. It was not her words, though. I thought that Mother was dealing with life the best she could, that things would not get better, and that she was progressing in her disease. Despite my "willing it to be," I knew that television was not the answer.

Word Play

Word play was an interesting "game" Mother and I often engaged in. Word play took a little time to learn, as there was no fixed "code" for the translation, and it could change quickly. I likened the "game" to an Enigma coding machine of World War II. Word play involved guessing the correct word to substitute within a sentence. For example, when Mother said, "I am just sitting here in my *motel*," it could be translated as, "I am just sitting here in my *room* (and will move back home, wherever that is, to where I will not be lost)."

Since the correct words were situational, it was helpful to know people, places, and things familiar to Mother to "win" at this game. Of particular interest was "Winnie." In real life, Aunt Winnie was the wife of Mother's brother Aubrie. "Winnie," however, seemed to take on a generic aspect—like a wildcard substitution—for the wife of someone such as a son, or even two sons. A brother and I tried to figure the connection. We suspected that since Aunt Winnie was an in-law, not a blood relative, any daughter-in-law might, therefore, be called "Winnie." But this was just a guess.

Word play also took on another form about seven months after Mother moved into Personal Care. The game expanded into idea or theme play. During one visit, Mother and I were having a conversation on our favorite topic, one where she and I could really relate: gardening. She was usually very clear about gardening issues and gave good, correct advice.

In response to my complaint of having trouble with getting green beans, Mother responded in a clear, positive tone: "Why don't you plant some more? They will mature and produce till frost."

"Have you ever planted bush green beans much?" I asked because I only remembered Mother planting half-runners. Here, the game got interesting.

"Your grandmother and I would plant running beans if we wanted a lot. But if you wanted to fill some gaps, then bunch beans would work," she said.

She sort of mixed *bush* and *bunch* and called it bunch, rather than bush, mostly. We then moved to picking blueberries, and Mother commented: "You know, we did not have blueberries back then. Our blueberries were huckleberries. They were little berries that grew on this vine, no I mean a little bush … bunch …"

With these words, something strange happened. After she said bunch, she immediately launched into a continuation of the bunch green beans. "You would plant two rows and you could have a good crop." The blueberry conversation was like it never happened, and the conversation moved uninterrupted and completely into green beans—apparently due to the word *bunch*.

Word play also included another, slightly different aspect, and more like fudging words. For example, Mother would say, "I do not take any medicine." I would respond, "Yes, you do. You take the same medicine as you have been doing for a long time." "I don't take any medicine," Mother would repeat. As Mother understood it, and I can agree with her, the staff *gave* Mother her medicine. Mother did not get up and open the bottles and *take* her medicine. Other than swallowing, Mother did not *take* any medicine.

Mid to Just Beyond

The neurologist had moved Mother to a three-month appointment schedule. Mother had now been in Personal Care for about seven months, and it seemed that in the last few weeks she had become less rather than more settled. I related to the doctor the episodes of frequent phone calls, word play, and wanting to go back home.

The doctor gave Mother a check-up, and I suspected he would prescribe a second medication, Aricept, for Alzheimer's, which has a different mode of action than Namenda. The doctor indicated that both medicines can and often are given, but he declined to give her the Aricept at this time. He showed an anguished expression and rubbed his head as he said: "Some think it is better to give the medicines early, but your mother is tolerating the Namenda well. I would not like to disrupt her. Let me know how she does and we will see."

I deduced from his demeanor and conversation that it was a difficult call, and he likely erred on the side of caution. I agreed with his decision because Mother was having such a good day and had once more "risen to the occasion" of the doctor's visit.

It *was* a good day for her—almost her best in recent days. So, during the wrap-up and realizing Mother would not understand, I asked, "Where is she?" referring to the stages of Alzheimer's. Without hesitation, the doctor said, "Mid to just beyond."

Knowing Herself

I told myself that my exploration of Mother's thoughts was for her own good, but I really did want to know how much Mother could reason about her life.

"So, Mother," I began on one visit, "when you say you feel like your sisters are setting up a visit, do you envision the visit now as you are today, or does it seem as if it is occurring back in your youth when everyone was back at home?"

Although the question was vague, Mother responded with a thoughtful explanation, clearly stated and clearly spoken—but she made no attempt to address my question. Instead, she talked about knowing people and growing up and personalities. So, I asked again. This time she struggled to find an answer.

"Why do you ask if *we* know about you?" I asked at one point. Was the "we" her three sons, her only living relatives? She seemed to put lot of stock in what *we* thought about her.

She looked surprised at my question.

"Do I say that?" she asked, almost ready to apologize.

"That is okay," I tried to reassure her, "but I just wondered why what *we* thought was so important."

Mother's response was clear this time and went to the heart of her soul: "You are my family and you know all about me."

Inherent also, it seemed, was the idea of order: everything was as it should be, we should all know the same thing, be in agreement, and have no dissension among us. This idea was an important aspect of Mother's philosophy from way back. At this time, however, the agreement was for reassurance that we knew her and would provide for her. She was quite childlike in this regard.

I was coming to the realization that this strong-willed, independent, do-it-all woman was losing these abilities and needed much reassurance and support. Maybe she always needed more support and I did not know it, but now it was clear that it was my turn to provide it. Mother and I were both in transition.

"What can I do to make you feel better?" I asked.

Her response reflected her philosophy and desires. "Well, sometimes I feel lonely, but I do not let it get me down. That is life, and I have been through many ups and downs before. You just get up and keep going and not let the bad times, or bad feelings, keep you down."

There was no doubt in my mind that this attitude had kept her going throughout her life. It was one of constant optimism.

When I commented on this, she looked at me and told me as honestly as she could, "That is the only way I can live." She gave the Lord credit for this. He seemed to have worked it particularly well within her background and personality. I was astonished that she still had this positive outlook when we visited, or at least on her better days. But I also knew that her optimism often lagged at night, when she was alone, and she called me in distress.

"Knowing thyself" played out in other aspects of Mother's life, such as her walking. Mother walked at least three times a day: after breakfast, after lunch, and after dinner. But why did she walk? "You do what you should," she said.

Mother's philosophy also caused some frustration. She did what she should, but she seemed to feel she should be doing more, although she could not. In correcting herself on a dull mind, she said, "It just takes more time to sort things out, to think things through." Sadly, the time had passed for her to ever really sort some things out. She knew how to live—after all, she has been doing it for more than 91 years. But at times this knowledge of herself seemed to get lost.

My strategy was to visit Mother a little before her dinner time, so that there was a natural stopping point, one that was so subtle Mother would not notice—or so I thought. As we finished our visit one day and I was about to leave, she said with a slight glint in her eye, "We may have to change this schedule of visits with your coming just before I have to go to dinner."

"How would we change it?" I asked.

"You could come earlier or come after dinner."

Mother seemed to know me pretty well, too.

The Air Conditioning Debacle

Not all my visits involved talking about Mother's deteriorating mental abilities. Some involved her living situation—which more than once was the cause of turmoil. Mother's apartment had a newly installed, digitally controlled heating/cooling unit and thermostat that worked very well. However, instead of setting the thermostat and leaving it alone, Mother liked to play with the controls when she was hot or cold.

In her old apartment she had played with the heating/cooling unit, turning it on when she wanted to and seldom allowing the thermostat to do its work. Before she left Independent Living, this fiddling with the temperature controls had become more problematic. I am not sure how long the air-conditioning episode had been going on in Personal Care, but it was approaching crisis state, both for Mother and the staff—and soon the problem would be mine.

Mother had not called me all day on this Friday, until about 8 p.m.

"I am so upset," she began "*She* seemed to be mad at me, and I have not done a thing to her."

It turned out that "she" was a staff member in Personal Care, and the "not done a thing" concerned the air conditioning.

"Did she say anything to you or act badly toward you?" I asked.

"No," Mother replied. "She didn't say anything. She just 'swelled up.'"

"Swelled up," as used by Mother, meant getting mad but not saying anything. Mother insisted that she had not done anything to be on the receiving end of a "swelling up." I tried to get some information about the thermostat over the phone, thinking I might avoid a nighttime visit. Getting any information, however, was impossible. After Mother became more settled—although I did not—she was finally able to tell me that the thermostat was set at 80 degrees. I asked her if that was comfortable.

After some back and forth, during which time she wanted to know if it was comfortable for me, we decided that 80 degrees was indeed comfortable for both of us. I made her promise to call me if she had more problems, but knew that I would need to make a visit.

Fifteen minutes later, I arrived at Mother's place. She asked me how far away I lived and how long it took to get to her apartment. This was a clue that Friday night had not been good. After refusing the apple she offered me two or three times, I went to the thermostat and explained what the numbers meant. The control was set to 80 degrees, the room temperature was 81 degrees, the unit was on the "cool" setting, and cool air was blowing in.

"Does it seem cold to you?" Mother asked.

I responded that the unit was blowing in cool air to bring the room temperature back down to 80 degrees.

"Oh yes," she replied. "Well, I have a quilt if I need it tonight."

I sat down for a minute to talk with her. Mother peeled an apple, one of several she had taken to her room from the dining hall, with a dinner table knife.

"Apples make you go the bathroom," she reminded me.

I said goodnight to her and walked to the staff desk to see what had happened earlier that evening. The two staff members on duty that night were frustrated. The air-conditioning debacle had occurred a few times and seemed to go as follows: Mother felt uncomfortable and played with the thermostat. When the cool air blew into her room, she felt cold and turned off the thermostat. The room got hot (with daytime temperatures of over 100 degrees), and she got hot but did not know how to set the controls. She called the staff, and they reset the thermostat. Then the cool air blew in and made her cold again, and the sequence repeated itself.

I recalled the nurse's story of when staff members had made three trips to Mother's room, and each time the thermostat was set on heat after the staff had turned it to cool. This night the staff said Mother had been down to see them about ten times, had grabbed a kitchen worker to fix her system, and had intercepted the pharmacy delivery boy to do the same thing. They were frustrated and mentioned more than once that there were only two of them to serve all of Personal Care. The unsaid part was that Mother had taken more than her share of their time and had taken it unproductively.

One of them said I should see the head nurse for some guidance on how to address the air-conditioning dilemma. Trying to stay on their good side (and in reality, believing everything they said), I asked them to call me if the problem continued.

As I commiserated to myself on the way home, I came up with a plan. I would tell Mother to leave her thermostat alone, and if it came on to go outside until it shut off. I held no illusions this plan would work.

Mother called again in a frantic state. She needed me to come over and see about her.

"What's wrong?" I asked, wearily.

"I don't know," she replied, "but I need someone to come over and take care of me."

When I arrived back at Personal Care, she was standing in the middle of her room, bewildered.

"I don't know what's wrong," she repeated to me. "I think I am going to have a heart attack. My heart is racing."

"You are not going to have a heart attack," I replied. "Sit down and tell me what is wrong."

As we talked, I realized the cold air was blowing, so I checked the thermostat. Aha! The temperature was set to 75 degrees, and the room felt the same with cold air blowing in.

"Have you changed your thermostat?" I asked.

"I have not touched that thermostat!" Mother insisted.

In fact, she denied ever touching it, except maybe once, some time ago. In a frustrated voice, I told her she had touched it and it was causing a problem with the staff.

"No one has ever told me that," Mother said firmly. She was most likely correct. The staff just came down, "swelled up," and reset the thermostat.

"Mother, you do touch it and often," I corrected her. "This touching the thermostat is a problem, and we need to find a way to change the situation."

The situation improved a bit when the nurse arrived to give Mother her eye drops. In a low voice, I inquired if Mother had come down to the desk about the air conditioning.

"Yes, one time," the nurse said, "but I do not know how to set it."

My guess is that when I was called to come over and "see about her," Mother had nowhere else to turn. She had been to the nurse for help, but she had been unable to fix the problem.

Did Mother even remember touching the thermostat?

Knowing that while Mother could not remember specifics such as names, times, or events out of context, she could still recall a name, time, or event if it popped up in conversation. I continued to remind her about touching the thermostat and letting it do its work. I even put a note on the unit with the words "Do not touch. Leave alone," hoping she would see the note and the words would jumpstart her memory and remind her of what to do—or rather, of what not to do. Then I went home and did not think about the thermostat for four days.

Unlearning Things

After Mother had been in Personal Care for about eight months, I discovered that the staff members were keeping a "rap sheet" on her. A spate of recent events, namely frequent requests to have her air conditioner set, in addition to requests for help with the phone and for walks outside the building aroused the concern of the head nurse. This rap sheet contained warning signs for patients with dementia and signaled the possible need for Mother to be moved to the Memory Care unit next door. We did not want to acknowledge that Mother was this far down the path of dementia. The nurse spoke to us with professional knowledge and personal experience; her father had dementia, and she was particularly concerned about Mother walking around outside, "She could walk out and not remember how to get back in."

The nurse was right, of course. I had experienced Mother's sudden drift in asking me where I lived and saying that she had never been to my house before, so I knew the loss of mental ability could be swift and unpredictable. The nurse went on to express the change in a memorable way, explaining that while children learn things, folks with dementia *unlearn* things. The question now was this: How long would it be before Mother unlearned so much that she needed to move to Memory Care?

The Walking-Outside Dilemma

When Mother told me she had a walking trail outside her building, I really thought she was imagining it, that it was word play, so I checked it out with the staff. When I asked if Mother really did walk outside, a worker responded: "I told her not to go outside when it is so hot, but she goes outside anyway and walks around."

Walking was something Mother had always done and resolved to continue. But walking outside became a real issue with real consequences. She could have an accident or forget how to get back inside the building. The rap sheet on Mother had disturbed all of us. We did not want her to go to the Memory Care unit just yet, but it was obvious that the staff and head nurse were watching and considering. With these concerns in mind, I said to Mother, "We need to stop walking outside."

She gave a funny expression, like she was about to say something but didn't know what. Finally, she put words to the expression and replied, "I have to walk. I have to get outside."

I thought Mother had just started walking outside the building a few weeks before. As far as I knew, her walks had always been in the hallways. I tried to be forceful: "We are concerned about your falling when you walk outside. The staff, the brothers, and I are all concerned," I added. I left off the part about not finding her way back in.

"You are?" she asked with surprise.

Mother lowered her head as if in thought and said, "Well, I don't want anyone to worry, so I just won't walk outside anymore."

I passed this positive agreement along to those concerned—that is, to the head nurse and my brothers. When I visited Mother the following day, I asked in an upbeat manner, "Have you had a good day?"

"Yes, I ate lunch and walked," she replied.

"Did you walk inside?"

"No, I walked outside."

"I thought we said we were not going to walk outside but stay inside?" I replied with some irritation.

She thought for a moment. "Did we say that? I do not remember that."

I launched into a monologue of our past conversation, our agreement to walk only inside, and the reasons for it.

"I just have to get outside," she responded.

Mother spent some time defending her need to walk outside. Her strategy seemed to vacillate between saying she was sorry and did not want to be contrary or hurt anyone, and telling me how she *had* to get outside. I was getting nowhere.

Later I found out from my brother that she had told him she had walked outside every day—even after our agreement. I was more than irritated now; I was mad. I am not sure if I was mad because she went against me or because I feared the next steps if she continued to walk outside. I said, "Mother, you are going to get us into trouble and maybe have to move. The staff is concerned about your falling and about, perhaps one day, not remembering how to get back in."

But Mother was not going to give up easily. After countering my argument with the defense that no one had told her she could not walk outside, and tearing up once or twice, Mother said coolly, "Let's both think about what to do."

Not so coolly I responded, 'I do not need to think about what to do. It is clear what to do. Walk inside and not outside!"

"I have walked outside all my life," Mother continued to insist.

"Mother, you have memory loss. Do you remember calling me this morning and then calling me right back because you did not remember you had already called?"

"Yes, yes I do remember," Mother said. "And I was almost sure I had called and started not to call you back."

"Mother, do you know that I have introduced you to the head nurse three times and you do not remember who she is?" I asked.

"Who *is* the head nurse?" Mother asked.

I wanted to scream.

"I think I do pretty well," Mother said. "I think my mind is okay. I read and remember things. I never thought I would get lost when I went outside. You know …" she paused, "sometimes, memory gets in your way and upsets you. Does that make sense?"

"Do you mean that memory loss is good sometimes because it keeps you from remembering things that upset you?" I asked.

"Yes," Mother answered.

The best I could tell, Mother's argument was that her mind was fine, that she had never intended or thought she would get lost, and that any memory loss she might have was good to keep her from getting upset. All of this just countered my argument and supported her need to walk outside.

I visited Mother again the next day before leaving on a four-day business trip. I was still miffed at her for misleading me, but the whole episode made me think: Did she not remember any of the initial discussion of walking outside? Did she remember our initial discussion and then *not* remember her promise? Did she remember all of it and just decide to do what she wanted to do?

I told her goodbye twice and that I would be back late Thursday night. Before I left, she had come out of the double doors to ask me if I would see her on Friday. I nodded yes and left. Before I had even arrived home, she had called wanting to say goodbye again and to thank me for taking care of her. I feared that I might have upset her and she, although acting calmly, might have really remembered some of our conversation.

A Meeting and a Test

I had all of Mother's mail delivered to my home so that I would be sure to see it all. I received a letter for Mother announcing a meeting for those living in Personal Care. I took the letter to Mother, told her what it was, wrote the date and time of the meeting on the letter, and left it for her on her desk. Two days later when I was visiting, I asked her if she remembered the letter and the meeting. I had a purpose: I was testing to see how bad her mind was. Mother's expression told me she did not remember the letter and certainly not the meeting.

"Do you know what it is about?" Mother asked me.

"I want to know if you know," I replied. "The letter and meeting are for you."

After some hem-hawing, she finally admitted she did not know.

I handed her the letter, and she held it and appeared to scan down the 20 or so lines. She gave it back to me without comment.

"Do you know what it's about?" I asked again.

"No, do you?"

It was obvious that she had not understood the letter. I told her there had been a survey among the residents, and the meeting was to discuss the results.

"Well, I do not have any comments. You know about two or three people run this place, and they do not need someone green like me to try to run it," Mother replied.

"It is just an opportunity to make suggestions," I offered.

"Well," she continued in a rambling way, "they do a good job and I am pleased."

"What about the lack of activities on Saturday and Sunday that you complain about? Are you complaining or just commenting?"

"Well, you know there are two or three that run this place, and they don't need to have everyone involved. They send those letters out because they have to."

For some reason, Mother did not want to involve herself in this matter. I pressed the point further until she agreed to attend the meeting. I did not care if she went or not—I just wanted to see how much of our conversation she remembered. It turned out later that she remembered nothing.

Although Mother had slid lower mentally, she still came up with another gem of wisdom that arose from my explaining to her the letter about the meeting: "Well, that is the way it is on paper," she said with fanfare. "That is not the way it is in life."

How many times have I dealt with an issue such as this but never expressed myself so clearly? I used Mother's words to clarify my thoughts several times over the next few days and beyond.

The First Confusion

It was the first confusion of a new kind: Mother confused her sons. She had called me three times since her supper at 6 p.m. I was in the garden and did not talk with her then, but at my wife's prodding, I called Mother about 8 p.m. The line was busy, as it was two more times. I figured she was talking to one of my brothers. I reached her on the fourth try. She was happy to hear my voice, as always, and I asked her if she had been talking to one of the brothers.

Mother said, "I was involved with the phone some." She never said who she was involved with on the phone. Later she said, "I called your older brother down at the place."

"What place?" I asked.

"Down … he was in his garden."

At some point, she asked if it was Dan she was talking to. I said yes, and she remembered talking to my wife earlier. She, and I, just passed over the garden bit. I thought surely that she had been talking to my brother earlier. That would explain her busy line and the confusion of him with me. So I called him to be sure. "No," he said, "I haven't talked to her today."

More evidence of this confusion occurred a week later when I found a note Mother had written on a sheet of paper: "Dan to go to Raleigh Friday to Monday." She had the date and place correct, but she had again confused me with my older brother. Additionally, the previous two nights had not gone well. She had asked for Aunt Audie's phone number and confused two of her sons. I thought back a year and realized how far Mother had declined. The discussions were now about how long Mother could stay in Personal Care and how we could afford Memory Care.

Walking Outside—Again

Before I got to visit with Mother, the head nurse called me aside for a word: "I saw your mother walking outside in the drizzle the other day. I watched her to be sure she got back okay. She went around the walkway and up to the road. Then she went around the big truck parked on the side of the road. She also gets very agitated about things, like about her trash can missing."

I went to Mother's room where she was waiting for me and was glad to see me, at least at first.

"Mother," I said sternly, "we need to talk."

"Okay," she responded. "Is there a problem?"

My voice gave away my concern. "Yes, Mother, you have got to stop walking outside. It is a real problem for the staff here, and they are worried about you."

"They are?" Mother asked, just as she had when I had told her the same thing two weeks earlier.

"Yes, we are all concerned about your safety and well-being. You have to stop walking outside."

The rebuttals came, just as before.

"I have to walk outside," she started.

"No, you don't!" I retorted. "You never walked outside until about two months ago."

"I feel like I am in prison if I cannot get out."

"You can get out all you want in the hallway. We encourage you to walk all you can *in the hallway*," I emphasized.

Then came the next rebuttal, a familiar tune: "They have never told me not to walk outside. I tell them I am going outside, and they say it is okay."

"Mother, you asked the kitchen staff. They do not have any opinion or authority on this."

"I do not believe that," she replied huffily.

We had finally come up against a major issue: Who was the boss?

But there was another angle to this story that had more complexities and consequences: The head nurse was pushing to have Mother go to the new dementia unit. While the fact that Mother had walked outside and around the road in the drizzle was a concern, in my view it was normal to be agitated over missing everyday things. It seemed to me that the nurse was pushing too hard. While the staff no doubt had Mother's interest at heart, I could not help but wonder how much of the pressure came from wanting to fill the new, empty, expensive dementia unit. (It later became clear that the staff saw a different side of mother's illness than we did.)

"If your mother needs to go there later and we do not have a room, then we cannot keep her here," the nurse explained.

This was the proverbial horns of a dilemma. We wanted to keep Mother where she was as long as possible because another move would be very disruptive to her. Her money was enough, with some left over for the time being, but a move to the dementia unit would pretty much take everything she had, so we needed a plan. Did she need to go now? Was there a chance that all the rooms would be taken when she needed one? Was it time for another move?

Walking Outside Still? You Bet!

Mother's insistence on walking outside continued to cause a stir. The walks seemed innocent enough. She used her walker and traveled a prescribed pattern each day, sometimes several times a day. She walked along the sidewalk up to the street, past any trucks or cars parked along the way, then walked back to the main area of the campus—about 400 feet total. She walked this path twice. She *promised* not to fall and to watch for cars. In her view, she could not be safer.

I had previously wondered if Mother remembered she was not supposed to walk outside or whether she remembered but was determined to do it anyway. I soon received my answer.

Mother said Saturday was a lonely day for her. I took her some flowers, and as I went to add water to the vase, Mother followed me into the bathroom. We talked about how her day had been, and she said it had been good.

Then she added, "I got up and cleaned my room, ate lunch, walked a bit outside (I thought I heard this comment at a lower volume), and just sat around." She repeated, louder this time: "I said I walked a bit outside. Did you hear me?"

"I heard you," I said, not looking up from the paper I was reading. I did not say any more about the walks.

When my wife and I visited the following Sunday, Mother again told us that she had walked outside, adding, "They don't like for me to do that, but I have this little walk and I go." Mother made walking outside sound not just innocent but something that really *should* be done. I stared hard at my wife, hoping she would burst into laughter. She did, but the arguments about walking outside were about to come to an end permanently.

As the weeks passed, and despite our protests, Mother kept up her walks outside, even though she was closing in on her last opportunity for independence. Mother had not yet wandered away into the woods or endangered herself or the staff, and Personal Care had no requirement for residents to stay indoors. For the time being, Mother had won!

The Next Move

On a Tuesday in early September, I visited Mother once again. As we sat and talked, the neurologist returned my call. I went to the bedroom, closed the door, and told him of her walking outside, her lostness, and other situations I could think of.

He focused his response on the walks. He was concerned that she was still going outside after I had asked her not to, since "wandering" can lead to a resident being asked to leave Personal Care. He prescribed a second Alzheimer's drug, Aricept. However, the dosage was half the usual amount, and I got the impression that this additional medicine might not help, and could even make the situation worse, but it was all we had left to try.

My brothers and I knew it was time we consulted with the head nurse about Mother, so we arranged to meet with her the next day. The question before us was: Should we move Mother to the dementia care unit *now*? We had been extremely fortunate in deciding moves for Mother as she required increased levels of care, but I was not hopeful that we would get this next move right.

Mother seemed fairly normal when we visited, and with family around she rallied to the occasion. While she could not remember recent things or events, such as what she had for lunch, she could talk in generalities, knew her family, and often gave good advice that came from 91 years of living. But the staff noticed things Mother did, unknown to us, that indicated dementia: Mother had shown up at the staff desk with dark rouge, or possibly lipstick on her eyebrows! While we saw, or wanted to see, the better side of Mother, the staff noticed her bizarre side.

Although we had been in denial about Mother's condition, her actions over the next few days convinced me that it was time for her to move to the Memory Care unit. We had already agreed with the neurologist that we would wait three months, until December, to see how the Aricept worked, but I was soon convinced that a move to Memory Care should be considered at the same time. The move would come at the beginning of the following year.

The next night Mother called several times, beginning just after her dinner.

"I am so lost," she began. "Will you help me understand myself? Is this my apartment?"

I tried not to answer the questions directly, to see where her mind was.

"Mother do you feel you are somewhere you can identify?" I asked.

"You said you would help me," she insisted.

I could see that Mother wanted to get right to the point. She did not want to be interviewed—she wanted answers, and answers now. She recognized her things (furniture, books, and so on) but still could not see the apartment as her home. But where was her *home*? Neither of us knew. She also admitted to walking outside, quickly adding she would not do that anymore.

The second call, which she knew was the second call, was much of the same.

The third call was similar. It became clear that the calls were a substitute for a visit. She kept me on the phone just to talk, but she really wanted me to come over. I did not.

Her lostness and its frantic consequences spilled over several times that week. Even on her good afternoons, I thought I saw less acuity and more fogginess. I was more than convinced that we should start preparing for the move to the Memory Care unit. I called one of my brothers to confirm that we were in agreement, then made preparations to move Mother again.

It Is Time

Sunday was a doozie. It was three in the afternoon, and I was home from church. I had just finished lunch when the fourth call came in.

"Dan," Mother began, "where *are* you?"

This was the usual greeting when Mother had tried to reach me and could not (or if the phone rang three times before I answered).

"Where is everybody today? Nobody is here with me. Nobody came to see me today!"

"Mother," I said rather sternly, "Who do you think is supposed to be there?"

"Well, I thought some of you (the family) were supposed to be here," she continued. "But, they're not! You don't have to 'jack me up.'" Mother used her familiar expression, which meant being told off or criticized.

"Who do you usually see on Sunday?"

She talked around the subject until I finally said, "*I* visit you, Mother. *I* visit you on Sunday."

Mother responded, "Yes, I knew you did, but I thought some others were supposed to be here." She was an expert at getting out of tight conversations.

I did not think the Aricept could have caused side effects so quickly, but Mother's confusion was growing. When I arrived at her apartment a short while later, Mother was asleep in her easy chair. I let her sleep as I glanced through the newspaper. After a while, I woke her so we would have some time to talk. I expected Mother to remember our slightly heated phone conversation, but if she did remember, it did not show. She was pleased to see me, as always, and acknowledged that she had taken a little nap. She asked if I had had a good day. Not once did she mention the conversation. Finally, I asked her if she remembered what we had talked about on the phone earlier that afternoon.

"Yes, I remember," was all she said.

Not willing to let it go that easily, I asked, "Do you remember calling me three times before?"

"Did I call that many times?"

Later, I found out that she had called one of my brothers about the same time as she had called me, but she never mentioned it.

"Was he (my brother) over here today?" she asked.

"No," I responded in a more civil tone. "He was not here. No one was here this morning,"

"It seems so real to me that he and I were doing something in the garden."

"Like hoeing weeds?" I asked.

"Yes, something like that. I guess I dreamed it," Mother explained. "Your dad and I were doing something together."

Mother had just transferred her reference from my brother to Dad. Now, it was Mother and Dad doing the work together. And to her it seemed so real.

Sometime earlier, the nurse had suggested that we accompany Mother on her walks outside—a point I had debated with my wife because I thought it would just encourage Mother to ignore our pleas to stay in the hallway. But now I capitulated to both women and asked Mother if she wanted to go for a walk outside. She excitedly agreed, and I let her lead the way because I wanted to see the path she would take. She did not go the way I was expecting (along the sidewalk up to the street, past the parked trucks, then back to campus). Instead, she stayed in the parking lot and commented, "I do not go up to the street."

I said nothing, but I let her continue to lead. She talked and talked and talked. It was all just pleasantries of how walking was good for you, how it made you stand upright, how you could see yourself as a shadow, and how she had learned this when walking back from the fields. It bordered on giddiness. I was amazed at how well she maneuvered her walker over curbs and around obstacles. We returned to her room as supper was being served. She thanked me again and again for visiting her, and was a bit weepy as I left.

I got a phone call that night at 10:30. This was the latest she had ever called, and I was asleep. "Where is your Dad?" Mother began. Even with all the other goings on, her question still shocked me. At first I did not answer but instead tried to talk around the issue. She let me do it this time, and we talked about things other than my telling her that Dad was not living. After a while, *she* mentioned that Dad was not living and that she must have dreamed all the events, whatever they were. She never said why she missed him, just "where is your Dad?"

The denial was gone—for all of us.

"My Mind Is Pretty Good, I Think. But It Might Not Be, and I Just Don't Know It"

I had already decided to visit Mother on Wednesday afternoon, even before the four phone calls I received before noon. Interestingly, two of these calls were on the house phone and two were on the cell phone. When I asked why she had called on the cell phone, she said she did not know she had done that. She said that she just called the number by the side of my name. She said she called just to stay in touch and to hear us and to know we knew where she was. There must have been seven or eight lists of all of her sons' phone numbers.

When I arrived, Mother was in the sitting room with two other ladies, her head buried in her newspaper. As soon as she saw me, she got up and asked her usual question: "Did you just come?" I never understood exactly what she meant by that, or if she used some of the words wrongly. I was in a questioning mood, and she was ready to talk. She said she had had a good day, a usual day. She had eaten breakfast and washed her dishes. I asked if *she* washed her dishes. She didn't handle the question well, as if she were afraid she would give a wrong answer. So, she hedged and hem-hawed a lot.

"Well, if I have just a few, I just wash them and put them away."

Finished with dishes, I moved on to the question of the television: if she didn't watch it, there was no need for her to have one when she moved to Memory Care.

"It frustrates me," Mother said.

I picked up on this point and asked, "Does it frustrate you to try to follow what the people on the television say, or …?"

"It doesn't frustrate me," Mother, replied, contradicting both of us.

I asked Mother again if she remembered being upset Monday night and calling me several times, then calling another son.

"Did I do that?" she asked.

"Yes," I said, "That's okay. I just wondered if you remembered."

"I remember talking to him sometime."

The pattern emerging was that she remembered bits and pieces of the conversation, but not the whole thing.

Then she said, "My mind is pretty good, I think. But it might not be, and I just don't know it."

"What *is* that?" was an often-asked question by Mother to me. "That" referenced some feeling or action she could not understand. It implied that I might know about her but that she did not. The broader part of the question, though, indicated a loss of confidence in herself, her ability to think, and her ability to make decisions—in essence, her ability to *be* and to *do*.

I knew Mother was losing interest in activities: She had not gone to Sunday School the past Sunday (just did not want to go, she said), and she did not watch television. Any material I brought her to read went unread. For example, the little history of her home community was put away never to be looked at again. It was frustrating, and clear to me that Mother was not as engaged as she had been just a short time earlier.

"You know, I used to be real busy, but not now," Mother sadly acknowledged as she realized she had mentally slowed. "I try to be interested in all they do here."

I felt as if Mother was willing this interest to be so, but her feelings were not that way. Although she tried to stay involved with all they did, she acknowledged that she wasn't. I could not let the opportunity pass without suggesting that more activities might be good for her, hoping to lead into a conversation about the move to Memory Care.

"I have no desire to do any more than I do," Mother stated firmly.

"Things just don't come to my mind quickly anymore," she said. Then for the first time I could remember, Mother said. "Maybe it's better not to live so long." This was the first time Mother had indicated that life was losing its appeal.

"Do you want to walk outside before I leave?" I asked.

"If you do," Mother replied, already getting up and preparing to go outside. Then she added, "I walked outside once today." I frowned at her. "I met a lady and told her I was not supposed to walk outside."

Well, I guess that made it alright, if she confessed it.

Mother walked the same route as Sunday, not going up to the street. She was steady as a rock. As we returned to her room and prepared for me to leave and for Mother to go to choir practice, she asked, "When am I going home? Oh, is *this* my home?" She seemed to remember just as she asked the question. When she called later that night, the first thing she said was, "Where am I?"

"You Will Be Given Words": Despair and Hope

The weekend in mid-September seemed to be the worst time for Mother so far. I was fed up and decided to do something about the incessant calls.

As I left to tell Mother my demands, my wife called for calmness and patience. I took her comments to heart to think about what I could say to change Mother's calling habit. Rather than thinking, I said a prayer about it. I thought of Jesus' instructions to Peter and the Apostles not to plan what to say, for the Holy Spirit will give you words (Luke 12:12). I was not going before the Sanhedrin, but I wondered if words would be given to me. I asked to see clear a way to help her, but I did not have a clue what that might be.

Mother was standing in the middle of her room, with a scowl on her face. She looked angry. I was angry, but I came with hope. We sat down to talk.

"Mother," I began, "we have to find a better way than your calling me all the time—several times a day."

"Do I do *that*?" Mother asked with great emotion. "I did not know I did that!"

"We have to find a better way."

"Oh, I so hate to bother my children," Mother replied.

I felt so sorry for her because she was fighting the dementia with no hope of winning. Mother felt guilty that she was such a bother. In her better days, Mother had done her share of taking care of the sick and aged. She knew dementia. She knew stress on families. Her mental capabilities were still enough to remember those afflicted, but now she was not able to stop herself from being a member of that group.

"Just throw away your phone number so I cannot call you," she demanded.

While it was tempting, I said instead: "No, Mother, that is not what I meant. I did not mean I never wanted you to call me. Call when you need to, but just don't call me several times a day."

Her next demand was even weightier: "Just put me in a nursing home. That's where people like me belong."

I saw a chance, and the words came to me: "Mother, there is a better place for you. We are not going to put you into a nursing home but into another place that you will like." I had been looking for an opportunity to bring up the Memory Care unit, and it seemed to have been handed to me on a silver platter.

"You are?" Mother said.

"Yes, it is close by, and it will be better for you and for me."

"Oh, let's talk about it another time," she said.

"Yes," I said, "another time."

While we tangentially hit on the "other place" a time or two, we held off on a full discussion. I was thinking I should follow up right away with the head nurse, and I left for home soon thereafter. No calls came that night.

On the next Sunday visit, I brought Mother fresh roses. She was asleep in her chair. When she awoke, it was with lots and lots of words about her condition and her loneliness, saying that she had never felt like this—the words just poured out. I listened because I did not think I could get a word in just yet, and further, I did not have anything useful to say. Somehow during all the verbiage about her condition, Mother spoke something that resonated: "When I get home, I am never going to leave again."

"Where are you now?" I asked. "Where do you think you are?"

She looked at me in a puzzled way and said, "I am in this room. I think I went away for the weekend."

"This is your home. This apartment is your home."

"No," she replied emphatically. "No, this is not my home. I hate this room."

I followed up. "Mother, where is home for you? If it is not a place, where is it?"

Mother then explained, "It is where my family is." Clearly, she missed being home and being with her family—a place that did not have a physical address.

I had already called the doctor to discuss taking Mother off Aricept while leaving her on Namenda. Unofficially, many internet bloggers talked about the side effects of Namenda when taken with Aricept: increased confusion, wanting to go home, crying, and loss of interest in other activities. This was very much Mother of late.

An Epiphany?

For a while after stopping Aricept, Mother was pretty good during the day, calling me just to "touch bases" and not talking for long. She admitted the need to hear family voices, and then she was off to walk or do something. At night, she was not as good, and her loneliness and confusion were worse. More often than not she would ask, "Is this is my apartment?" and, "Who lives with me?" She wondered why no one had come to visit. While I felt for her, I fell into the trap again of trying to work out problems rather than just listening.

At some point, the thought came to me (and should have come earlier) that I was trying to reason with Mother and explain her behavior, giving explanations of confusion and loss of memory. A better approach would be to say, "Let's talk a while and maybe you will feel better." After all, that is what she wanted: connection to her family. She seemed to fear that everyone had forgotten about her and did not know where she was.

My epiphany was that I needed to just listen and talk to Mother about nice things, rather than ask her questions to try to understand her behavior. I promised myself to try this, but I knew I had be on guard or I would revert back to tests, questions, and strategies, which were useless. *Listening* would be my next plan of action.

"I Feel Defeated"

"I just feel defeated." Mother said. "Defeated!" she emphasized.

Mother was falling further into dementia, and she realized her mind was not good. My theory was that Mother thought she could "will her way" out of this, and that her mind would eventually get better. But her confusion and loss of memory were not getting better. Mother could not reason things out or think things through or will them to be the way she preferred. Nothing helped. I was not sure if she gave up television, writing, and so forth because of her dementia or because it was just too easy to do nothing.

"I am so lazy," was a refrain she liked to use. Her tone suggested that she would try to change and do better, but in Mother's case, nearing 92 and suffering from dementia for more than a year, it was just that: a refrain. The most consistent activity Mother was involved with (at least as it appeared to me) was calling one, two, or all three of her sons—and calling often.

Mother's opening statement was always, "I am just calling to touch bases."

Because she could not remember when or whom she had called, it was impossible to keep a record. As the calls increased in number, Mother's opening statement became more honest.

"I am so lonely that I just wanted to hear your voice," she would say. Then her feelings of defeat led her to comment, "This place is pretty boring, with not much to do."

"Mother," I said, "they have all sorts of activities and games, and meals."

Mother's reply was classic: "Well, I do not want to do what everybody else does. I like to have some time to do what *I* like to do."

She may have been arguing with me and trying to establish her position. Defeat seemed to take many forms.

We thought about a way to help Mother by having her write her thoughts down. I had also bought her a diary book several months earlier, mostly for me to write notes when visiting. A brother was actually ahead on this; while we were away camping for a few days, he had brought her a pad and encouraged her to write things down. So, while the idea had been present, no one had actually pressed the point, until now. I was pleased to see her writing such things one Sunday when I dropped in to visit, so the next idea was to facilitate these writing sessions. One way was to get her a writing table to hold on her lap. I am so lazy, I thought. I need to go out and get that table.

Wrinkle Cream

Mother did read some things, I discovered. She had alluded to the wrinkles on her face a few times before. An ad in the newspaper caught her eye, and she began reading the company's advertisement, which stated: "Ugly lines gone in 90 seconds." The ad continued: "Miracle beauty breakthrough makes wrinkles disappear from view instantly. See for yourself. Free."

As she read this ad, I watched her as she focused intently on the words.

"That lotion must really work. See what they said," Mother posited.

I told her it was an ad, not a report, put out by the company that makes the product.

Mother countered, "It must be good or they would not say these things."

I repeated that it was an ad put out by the company to convince people to buy their product. I could see by her look that she did not believe me. I expected a request to get some of that magic lotion.

Mother seemed to particularly like the "testimonial," and read it out loud: "It felt like weeks since we'd been alone, but last weekend we snuck away for a romantic night out. No kids. No TV. Just an intimate dinner for two. So I knew this was the night for *Instant Effect*. Before we even left the house, he gave me *the look*, which I haven't seen in a long time. 'Wow,' he said. 'You look amazing.' Then he got real close, and stayed close all night."

I felt uncomfortable sitting there as Mother read about the man's obvious desires and intentions, and the woman's delight in them. Did Mother understand? Oh yes, I think so. And she seemed to enjoy the intimations throughout the claims.

"Well," Mother concluded with a smile, "I guess it really works."

What was my Mother thinking?

Should We Tell Mother?

The idea that we should tell Mother she had Alzheimer's disease was weighing on my mind. We had thought it best not to, for we did not know how she would handle such information. It might be devastating. An alternative view was that she would then know the cause and not worry over "What is wrong with me?" or in Mother's words, "What *is* that?" I tried to find some middle ground.

"Mother, you have serious memory loss," I said. "I have noticed it for several months. It is not going to get better. We have to learn new strategies to deal with memory loss."

"Did anyone in your family suffer memory loss?" one brother asked Mother.

"Well, my brothers, and my sisters," Mother said as usual in her platitudes without revealing any real information. I think my brother then specifically mentioned Aunt Lilly. Still, Mother would not, or could not, give any specific recollection. The question remained: Was she avoiding the obvious, or did she really not know?

I wore out my welcome with Mother that day. I hounded her with turning on her television and writing down her thoughts. Why did I do it? I do not know, for I was beaten at every turn. Maybe it is the nature of a scientist's approach, to question and to seek answers, but in this case, there were no answers. We talked, we strategized, we planned, and we even wrote down ideas, but I dare say I had not left her room before all our work was forgotten. I wanted Mother to be able to do more than she did—to turn on her television rather than calling me when she was lonely—but, she would not. She had no desire to improve. She was tired. She was defeated. She was old. She had dementia.

"I Am Old"

Our next strategy was to tell Mother her problems were related to her age. She dwelled more and more on the idea of getting old until *she* began to offer it as an explanation for her confusion and memory loss. I could not say that Mother was happy about it, but "getting old" did permit us to move to another topic of conversation.

Then I noticed on our visits that the subject of her getting old came up more and more frequently. It seemed as though Mother was accepting the getting old idea and the fact that she could not and *did* not have to do everything. Still, there were times when she would say, "When I get over my sickness, I have got to do some things." During her worst delusions she seemed to think she would go back home, but lately, she was more comfortable with "getting old"—a fact that seemed to bring some relief. Any strategy that offered some relief was used; I adopted one on explaining why she "left home."

"Mother," I began, "do you remember how badly you felt before you left your home? The house needed a lot of repair, and you did not sleep at night worrying over all the things that needed to be done."

"Yes," Mother replied, "I do remember that."

I continued, "Here, you have all these people to assist you and care for you. And you pay for this (this fact was important for her to know). So, you can just relax and live."

Mother was at times somewhere in between "here" and "back there." In her mind, she was adjusting, but sometimes she tired of adjusting.

"How Far Away Are You From Me?"

Mother would frequently ask, "How far away are you from me?" I would tell her, not always as patiently as I should, that I lived about three miles away from her. Her other sons lived about one and a half hours away. What she really meant, however, was: "Who of my family is near me, or am I alone?"

Mother feared being lost or alone, and that was the reason she wrote all of our phone numbers on many, many sheets of paper. She wrote them, neatly, I might add, on any note or letter that came to her. Often, after I told Mother where my brothers were, she would ask again how far away from her I was. She seemed to want to hear it again and again for reassurance.

Perhaps related to the fear of her being "lost" was Mother's need to know where we all were. My brother's hunting trip to South Dakota really threw her. First, she could not keep straight when he was going and returning. Then, it seemed that his leaving resulted in Mother feeling we had all gone away and that she was alone. The same problem arose when I was to be away for a few days. "All my family is gone," Mother would cry.

As her condition worsened, her obsession with knowing where we all were and how far away from her we were grew, becoming quite restrictive. I began to resent Mother wanting to know what I was doing, as though she wanted to know why I was not with her. On her worst days, she would call four or five times during the afternoon and begin with, "Dan, are you home?" or "I did not think I would get you at home." One time, she said, "When I get better, I won't do this."

I told her she would not get over it; it would be like this from now on. She had Alzheimer's, and neither Mother nor I knew the way forward.

Thanksgiving and Confusion

Thanksgiving that year and the days afterward did not go well for Mother. We were going to be visiting my brothers and their wives, a 90-minute drive from Mother's apartment. The day started on a dodgy note when Mother asked where she was going to live after this trip. I told her that we would return to her home there. She was confused and admitted that her mind was not working well that day.

"My mind is a little foggy, and I don't know why. I will be happy when I am over this," Mother said too many times to count. She called my wife "Winnie." As soon as we arrived, Mother became confused. During the Thanksgiving meal, Mother turned to me and asked, "Is Dan coming?"

"Mother, *I* am Dan!" I replied.

"Oh yes," she laughingly said, then turned to my wife and asked, "Did Dan come alone? Why didn't his wife come with him?"

We were all too surprised to respond.

After we ate, we wrapped Mother in a blanket on the sofa as she was obviously cold. Typical of Mother trying not be a burden, when we asked her if she was cold and wanted her jacket, she replied, "Are you cold? Do you need a coat?" Mother did not want to be different or draw attention to herself. It was always hard to give something to Mother without receiving something back. Even in her dementia, she still lived that way. In this, she was still Mother.

On the way home, Mother asked where her suitcase was. We told her that she did not bring a suitcase, and the conversation moved to why she did not have it. A few minutes later she again asked where her suitcase was. When we arrived at her home, she asked if we were there yet, which was understandable since it was dark and we had parked in a different place. She asked us to stay the night, as if we had a long way to go. I explained we lived only a few miles away.

The trip away from her home caused the confusion of the next two days. The following day, Saturday, Mother kept asking who was coming to see her or where everyone was. It seemed that she had had a flashback to the day before and was confused because her boys were not around. "Weren't they coming to see me?" she asked again and again. "When am I going home?" She had been transported to a place with her family, but they were all of a sudden gone.

Sunday was worse. Mother called me on my cell phone at Sunday School. When I could break away, I called her and said, "Mother, I am in Sunday School." What I meant was, "Mother, don't call me when I am tied up like this. You know better than that." She apologized for calling me, but she had such anguish that she was bound and determined to contact me, no matter what. Before we got home from church, she had called the house another three times and my cell phone once. I knew she was at lunch, so I waited for her next call. It came 30 minutes after we got home.

On my Sunday visit, I was bombarded with a host of questions: "Where is everyone? I cannot find anyone. Where am I? Where do I live? Where do you live? How far are you away from me? Are we the only ones here? Where are my sons? Where is Audie?"

Finally, I reminded her, "Mother, you have a disease in your brain." Her expression was not one of horror, but more of gentle surprise.

"Is it my old age?" she asked.

"It is more than old age," I said. "You have a disease in your brain that causes memory loss and confusion."

"Does everyone know this?" she asked, obviously concerned about how she was viewed by others.

"Yes, of course they do."

"Did you know this?"

"Yes, I have known for a while."

"How long have I been this way?"

The questions were flying out as Mother tried to analyze her situation. I told her everything but without using the word Alzheimer's.

"Thank you for telling me," said Mother. "I needed to know this."

The neurologist had told us that familiarity was important, and we had experienced the value of routine. By violating this routine at Thanksgiving, we had brought on much confusion. The neurologist also told us that whenever an Alzheimer's sufferer experiences an illness or event that causes decline, likely they will not fully recover to the previous state.

A Doctor's Visit, But No Relief

At the doctor's visit in December, the neurologist did not want to try another medicine after the Aricept attempt. He was not sure if Aricept had caused the increased anxiety, but the Namenda regime was adequate. He said that she seemed to have reached a plateau, or at least was mentally declining very slowly. I told him that I told Mother she had a brain disease but did not mention Alzheimer's. He agreed that, in his view, I should not say the "A" word. While confusion and loss of memory is bad, the word Alzheimer's has a stigma that could be further detrimental.

The doctor offered comments about his own mother, who had dementia also. "She calls several times a day, and if she cannot reach us, she gets very anxious," he said. His description was *my mother*.

He said that his mother talked about home a lot and got confused when out of her routine. When she was away from her home, she kept looking at her watch, knowing dinner was to be served at the home soon. As I related to the doctor our Thanksgiving trip and Mother's confusion as to where she was going and where she was returning, he nodded. He confirmed that taking her away from her home for even a night was not a good idea.

I had to ask, "Doc, can we do anything more for her?"

He shook his head.

Beginning the Move

The call came from the Personal Care nurse: "Your Mother needs to move to the dementia unit."

The staff had found Mother wandering in the dining room and on the fifth floor. She said she did not know the way to her room. (Her previous room in Independent Living had been on the fifth floor). She had a banana in her hand and did not know they would prepare food.

My brothers and I were torn. We did not want to move Mother too quickly, but we did not want to wait too long either. We knew Mother had to move soon—her erratic actions were well known to the staff, although not to us. This, and Mother's constant lostness and incessant phone calls, convinced us that now was the time. A move, however, is not quite that easy. Many arrangements have to be made and signed off by a doctor. According to the head nurse, it would be a matter of days or a few weeks at most.

For Mother's sons we hoped a new move would bring Mother into closer contact with other residents and the staff, more frequently and more intimately. I figured Mother was craving social interaction, and she had very little where she was now. A more communal environment, we hoped, would give her more pleasure. Such an environment would give *us* more pleasure if she did not call so often. Maybe she would not be so lonesome. Maybe she would feel better. In all this, though, I failed to realize the importance to Mother of *family*.

Birthday Number 92

I really did not think we would celebrate this birthday. Mother was in excellent physical health; however, mentally, she was getting worse. I did not know what another year would bring, but here we were. Mother had been in Personal Care for more than a year. We bought red roses and a cake decorated with "Happy #92." On Mother's birthday, we brought the cake over for dessert for all the residents. Mother was pleased and acknowledged "Aubrie and Winnie" for bringing the cake over. We just nodded in agreement. Everyone seemed to enjoy it—one person even told Mother "Happy Birthday," and Mother beamed.

After lunch, as people were leaving, Mother stood up, waved her left hand over the crowd in a regal way, and thanked everyone for coming in a dismissal of the group. But no one was listening. She walked over to say something to the two men left at the men's table, but they were talking and ignored her or never heard her. Mother's 92nd birthday did not seem to interest them. That evening, and after several phone calls, Mother wondered where everyone was and who was spending the night with her.

What Do We Discard?

Having made the decision to move Mother once again, my brothers and I began to think about how to do it. She would have little space in her new room, and the closet was tiny. There was only room for about a tenth of the clothes in her current closet. Some people had already offered that this was an opportunity to throw away stained garments and bring out some new ones that had never been worn. We wondered what Mother was saving them for, but this was just her conservative nature.

I began preparing Mother for the move by telling her she would move to a place where there were people, more activities, and more interaction.

I said, "You will like being over there."

"Where is that place?" Mother asked.

I knew she would ask that question, but I did not know what to call it. Not the dementia unit, or worse, the Alzheimer's unit.

So, I said "The new place, where they have more care, and a brand-new room."

Of course, what I did not say was that the room was smaller, the closet *much* smaller, and the doors would be locked at all times. I thought those comments could wait. Mother seemed excited when I told her about more care.

The next day she was less thrilled, and stated that she enjoyed being where she was. She was already getting cold feet. I knew that getting her ready would take more time. Mother said that she liked her room and her furniture. I wondered if she was laying down the gauntlet for what she would take with her. I was more than ready for Mother's next move. The phone calls had gotten more frequent, coming almost every night. But when the calls were less frequent, I worried then as to why she did not call. One night I even *dreamed* Mother was calling.

About a month before Mother's move, it seemed that every night was a terrible time for her. Often, she would call several times. She would carry on about not reaching everyone, as though she had to know where all her sons were. This was particularly frustrating for me since I did not want to tell her where I was or what I was doing all the time. I felt she was imposing, but I did not tell her that.

I made a routine of answering about three or four calls a day and letting the phone ring the other times. Usually, she would not leave a message but hang up just before or after the voicemail picked up.

Sometimes the calls were short with the comment, "I just wanted to hear your voice." Sometimes there was a full-scale conversation about herself, her plight, her loneliness, and sometimes her lostness. It was always about her and her situation. My brothers indicated the same, and they, too, began not taking all her calls. While we had hopes that her new home would provide more entertainment and socializing for her, there was no guarantee there would be fewer phone calls to us.

Mother's dementia seemed worse at night. Often her focus was on Audie. But her comments began to be a bit more bizarre than just asking where Audie was and whether she was dead. One night Mother said she needed Audie's phone number. I asked why. Mother replied, "I just wanted to talk to her and see how she was doing." I paused for a moment, and then Mother said, "Audie is dead, isn't she?"

Damn You, Alexander Graham Bell!

For Mother, the telephone was her lifeline. For me, it was the bane of my existence. I tried to convince Mother to be more involved with her community there rather than trying to keep up with her sons. She said she did *not* try to keep up with all of us, and that she just called because it made her feel good to hear our voices.

On my next visit, Mother sensed that I was upset and asked, "Why are you upset? What do I do that upsets you?"

I replied, "You call too many times a day. You call me 20 or 30 times a day. And if you can't get me, you get concerned about where I am."

With quivering chin and weepy eyes, she said, "The last thing I ever want to do is upset my children; I love them more than I love myself." Then the clincher, "I would rather *die* than hurt any of my children."

Oh boy. The gauntlet had been laid down.

I was not feeling so noble now, just more angry. "How many times do you need to hear my voice?" I asked.

The reason she called was not a big deal to Mother. She called because she wanted to. "If you do not want me to call, I will not call again," she offered, as she wrote down a statement to that effect on her notepad. "I will not call unless it's an emergency or I want to, in which case I will ignore what you said. If that is what you want, that I not call you, that's the way it will be."

She looked me square in the eye and did not blink.

"Mother," I began, "we just want you to be happy. I know you get anxious when you call and you do not reach us."

Mother replied, "I am happy with what I am doing and the way I live."

Finally, out of frustration, I told her she was *not* happy. She complained all the time about being lonely and lost. Mother's comeback was classic: "Sometimes you just talk to make conversation. You need something to talk about."

"But if you don't mean what you say," I replied, "if you are just saying stuff that doesn't matter, how can I believe you? How can I help you?"

After a few more rounds of this, I told her I had to leave. I was frustrated and wanted Mother to know it. I had "swelled up." But I cleaned her glasses first and told her I was going on a trip for about a week. She lowered her head as if saddened I was leaving. But she did not say anything. I repeated this a moment later, and she wished me a good trip. I kissed her, told her I loved her, wished her a pleasant rest that night, and then left. She said she loved me.

I left with a lot of guilt. I forgot my epiphany to listen more often and had tried again to use reason and logic. I had upset Mother and made her unhappy. At home, I regretted my actions and felt the guilt.

Later, the phone rang. It was Mother.

"Dan, were you over here tonight?"

"Yes, Mother, I was there and brought you a Valentine's gift—a flower."

"Was I here when you came over?"

She didn't remember I was there when she called the next two times, three minutes apart. My guilt lessened.

Mother celebrating her birthday in Memory Care with sons Elmer, Frank, and Dan.

Chapter 3
Memory Care

Shrinking to Fit into Memory Care

The new staff was also gearing up for Mother's move. The activities director and head nurse came to get Mother for a test run of events; the effort did not go well. Mother, although pleasant, suddenly refused to cooperate and asked to go back to her room. The way the staff described it was as though Mother thought the nurse and activities director should not be there without her son's approval. I knew all of this before the nurse called me because Mother had been on the phone as soon as she returned to her room. She was distraught and confused about where she had been and why. She told everyone that she had been in Personal Care but just a few days.

The week before the move to Memory Care is a time I would like to forget. I hated the calls. I did not want to talk to Mother, and I could not wait until we got her moved. Our plan for the move was to remove Mother from the premises altogether while we transported her furniture and personal possessions to Memory Care—but we were doomed from the start. When we arrived at the home, breakfast was still going on, and unless Mother was in a hurry, she lingered in the dining hall with the others.

While Mother ate, we began the first order of business: taking apart the bed and emptying drawers. One brother got there later than the rest of us, about the same time that Mother returned to her room from breakfast. I cannot remember Mother's exact words, but our presence there caused her to recollect that it was moving day. She was not upset, which was a welcome sign. My brother was able to get Mother to take a seat in the sitting room, but we later decided to take her to the beauty salon to have her hair done. As it turned out, this plan was good—that is, until we forgot to collect her. A lady found Mother wandering the hallways and brought her to her apartment. We were pleased, but just wished it had been a little later.

"What's going on?" Mother exclaimed as she came in. "No one told me I was moving."

We continued the move, debating what to take since space was at a minimum. Mother's new space in Memory Care was a single room with one closet. The only furniture we moved was her bed, a table and lamp, a recliner, and one chest. All the other furniture was given away, except the few things kept in the family. Photos and some of her teapots and other such items were displayed on shelves. Later on, the retirement center loaned her a television that had been purchased for promotional purposes. And her phone? Well, we did not move her phone. And there was no discussion

All that was left were her clothes, which had to fit into the tiny closet. A few days before the move, I had suggested that we go through everything and get rid of all she did not wear. Mother rejected the idea of culling her clothes outright. No one was welcomed to pick through

Mother's clothes. We ended up putting a few clothes into the closet and stowing the rest in a storage room.

Outside Mother's room was a locked glass display case where we placed pictures of family members and some of her ceramic items from home. I was not sure she ever noticed them. I was still feeling the pain of the previous weeks and wanted to leave as quickly as possible. I ran some errands for Mother.

The brothers stayed for a while longer, with one brother hanging around until her supper time. He was trying to comfort her and explain the situation. While I am sure Mother was pleased that he was there, I doubt any words were meaningful or remembered. I had returned to my epiphany that explanations did not work and we should find a pleasant subject to discuss. In Mother's case, this subject would be her family and when she would be back home.

I began to feel relief when I realized that Mother was moved and there were nurses and staff to take care of her 24/7. And, she did not have a phone.

Settling In

Mother's room was on the "green" side of the Memory Care unit. The sleeping rooms, which consisted of a 12'x12'-foot living space, had a spacious bathroom with a shower. Two mirror-image sides of 17 sleeping rooms—one painted green, the other yellow—surrounded their own television room, nurses' station, dining room, and kitchen. A common activities room and outside garden separated the green and yellow suites. The brightly painted and spacious ceiling reflected much sunlight. The smells and sounds of a nursing home were absent; it felt safe, comfortable, and orderly.

The question on most folks' minds was how Mother was settling in to her new home. My question was: Will the phone ring again? In fact, when the phone did ring (and it was not Mother), I still cringed. But she did not call the first day or so. I was told that staff there used anti-anxiety medicine a lot. Mother had gone to the desk and asked the nurse to call me. She had a list of phone numbers in her hand. As promised to me, the nurse was able to distract her and get her into a more positive frame of mind. I do not know how many times this happened, but the head nurse kept telling me how many pages of phone numbers she found on Mother. I was given four pages. At one point, the nurse said Mother brought a phone book and pointed out my name to the staff. Mother's action could have meant that the nurse had *all* the pages of phone numbers. We were not sure yet, but it did show how resourceful Mother could be. Per staff instructions, I did not visit the first week to let Mother adjust, but she was on my mind a lot.

On Saturday, I received the dreaded phone call, and it resulted in a confrontation. The nurse was new, and it was her first day on the job. Mother found a weak link in the armor and struck. The new nurse told me that Mother would not take her medicine until she spoke to me. This was a novel approach and possibly one well thought out. Maybe we had underestimated Mother. Before I even spoke to Mother, I told the new nurse that she was not to allow

Mother to call. The nurse apologized, not aware of the tension that the excessive phoning had created between us. I spoke harshly to Mother, telling her I needed time away and that she had consumed my time for the last several weeks. Mother, to her credit and strength, did not back down. I told Mother I was angry with her for calling. Mother told me she was angry with me. I told her I was not coming over to see her.

Mother said, "Get yourself over here and see about me now!"

"No!" I said, and hung up.

It was less than 10 minutes before I called the nurse back and asked her if I really needed to come over. She said Mother had taken her anti-anxiety medicine and was calming, but it would be good if I came over. When I arrived, I tried to show as much displeasure with Mother as I could. Mother was so proud to see me, crying softly and wanting to hug me. I was anxious to get to the heart of the matter. Mother and I went into her room and sat down. After her usual questions, the tension eased, and we discussed matters more calmly. She did not give an inch. Mother knew what she wanted and would not give up. She used all her resources: kindness, flattery, and appeal.

I had to admire Mother. She had managed to breach the phone barrier, she had me present, and now she wanted to discuss the next subject, which was herself and her condition. After we had gone through her litany of questions again, starting with, "How far away from me are you?" I told her I was sorry, that none of this was her fault (which she agreed with), but that I did not know what she wanted me to do. Mother knew I was upset, and I had mistakenly described Mother as a "problem." In any event, the misspoken word "problem" stuck around.

"I am not a problem," Mother said more than once. "I participate in what I should."

Mother continued to defend herself. She desperately wanted us to be in agreement—that she was not a problem and in fact that there was not any problem at all. I repeated that I did not know what she wanted me to do.

Mother then said, "I do not want you to do anything."

"Do you want me to just sit here while you ask me the same questions over and over and over?" I asked. "I have told you the answers, but you cannot remember. What do you want me to do?"

Mother had no answer. I had no answer.

Obviously, some type of transition had to occur, so I thought I would play Mother's game of "willing things to be."

"I do not see a problem," I said, "Nothing is wrong. Do you see anything wrong?"

Mother replied, "I do not see anything wrong."

While I knew what the matter was, and I suspect Mother did too, we were able to skirt around the anger and tension, agreeing that it must have just been a misunderstanding. This magic word, "misunderstanding," seemed to calm all the issues. No one was at fault, no specific sin was named, everyone saved face, and we were all in agreement. So, we left it as a misunderstanding. We left as somewhat friends, but I still cringed when the phone rang that evening.

A Slow Adjustment

After the few days of adjustment given to Mother, I began visits again. No matter when I visited, Mother's question was the same: "How far away from me are you?" Mother still feared she would be forgotten. My wife and I visited her about 10 days after she had moved into Memory Care, and I visited her a second time the following Sunday and took some supplies: toothpaste, shampoo, dental floss, and mouthwash. The staff dutifully marked her name on all the items.

This visit did not begin well. First, Mother wanted to know where I had been, suggesting I should have been there with her. I ignored her, but she asked again. I began putting her toiletries away and continued to ignore her. Finally, she thanked me and said I would *have* to answer her.

I turned to her and said, "I have been at home."

I hoped my statement answered her question, but more than that, I hoped it said that I would not be subject to being there all the time. I promised myself not to get angry or confrontational that day.

The head nurse thought Mother was adjusting well, although the staff indicated that things weren't always calm. A staff member intercepted me before I left and asked if she was not supposed to let Mother use the phone. Before she even finished the question, I said that indeed Mother was *not* to call. I might even have added "ever." I am pretty sure Mother had given her contradictory orders, but the staff member had followed my request. Another staff member told me to write down on a pad that I had been there that day to counter Mother's refusal to believe I had visited and that "the staff should call me."

The third time I visited, Mother was just finishing a puzzle. She was so happy to see me. My wife had suggested that I should take Mother outside for a walk and not just sit and listen to Mother's questions. We walked down the sidewalk past the entrance to her old room in Personal Care. Mother recognized it. She commented that she used to live there. Sometime later in the conversation, she mentioned a phone, not having one, and wondering when they would install it.

Mother asked, "Would you like to talk to them?"

I declined and let it drop. Thankfully, Mother did too. That was the first time she had mentioned not having a phone.

While I sat with Mother in her room after our walk, I thought about what to do to occupy her mind. I wrote in her book that I had been with her that day and some other stuff that she asked about. I filled up a page and realized as I turned to start a new one that Mother had written items in two days before. The writing was slanted but very neat. I read her the news in the paper that day. Then I had this brilliant idea: Why didn't I read to Mother when I came over? I began to think of things she might want to know about or remember.

Departing after my third visit was not a smooth exit. As I tried to pull away, Mother found many important questions to ask. A staff member realized the situation and said she needed my signature. Mother said she would wash her hands for supper while I signed, then the staff member let me out the secure door. I was glad not to be in that staff member's shoes.

The Signs of Caregiver Stress

I came across a card I had collected from the Alzheimer's Association that read: "Pass this along to a caregiver you know!" I read through the 10 signs of caregiver stress, and two hit home.

The first was "denial about the disease and its effects on the person who's been diagnosed." This denial was likely present among all three of Mother's sons. We had seen Mother's dementia progress, and the doctor had told us that she would only get worse—but we were in denial about how far along Mother's disease really was. My brothers and I would discuss how "clear" Mother was that day. She was clear, we know now, because some of us were there. We saw her in her very best state. What we did not see, however, was Mother's bizarre behavior, monotonous questions to the staff, and her wandering around Personal Care. Even on good days Mother could not carry on a conversation or recall details, and in the middle of a conversation she was likely to ask, "Where is Audie?"

The second sign was "anger at the person with Alzheimer's or others that no effective treatment or cures currently exist and that person does not understand what's going on. *If she asks me that question one more time, I'll scream.*" I confess to this one too. The major cause of my frustration until we moved Mother to Memory Care was that I could not do anything to help her other than be at the end of the phone listening to the same questions as always. I had no answers. A lot of the tension ended when Mother went into Memory Care and the phone calls stopped. She still repeated questions on visits, but it was manageable and began to evolve after a while to a more pleasant time for both of us.

One Month In

I purposely did not visit Mother much right after her move to Memory Care, and the first few visits did not go well. Sunday in late March of Mother's first month there was a particularly low day. It began with a phone call from a brother, who had received a call from Mother at eleven that morning. He was a bit frantic. The nurse on duty had said it was still a while before Mother could take her scheduled Xanax, and she was very anxious.

The first instruction from my brother was to the staff: "Don't wait. Give the medication!"

The second instruction was from Mother to my brother: "Get yourself over here and take me home now!"

He did not know what to do next. The staff had told him that they knew Mother was not supposed to call us, but they had no alternative that day. I told my brother I had planned to see Mother on Sunday afternoon as usual but would go over earlier—a visit I now dreaded. I had been away that week and had not seen Mother since the previous Sunday. I knew she was anxious and had demanded to be taken home. Even though my expectations were low, when I walked into her room, I was flabbergasted; her bed was loaded with pictures from her walls, toiletries from her bathroom, and clothing from her closet. Mother was packing to leave.

"Mother, what are you doing?" I asked, in a voice just a little lower than a scream.

"I thought it would be easier to carry the chests out," Mother replied calmly.

"Carry them where?" I demanded.

"I thought we were going home."

"What home, Mother? This is your home. You do not have another home!"

Still calm, Mother asked where my brother (the one she had called) was.

"He is at home," I said.

Mother continued, "Is he not coming over?"

It appeared as though Mother was wondering where all her movers were to take her home. I wished I could handle these situations better than I did.

I was upset with Mother and managed to make her upset with me. I don't know why I said the things I did, such as accusing her of laying a guilt trip on me. I had completely forgotten my plan to just listen to Mother without trying to explain the situation to her. The definition of insanity is doing the same thing over and over and expecting a different result.

After the argument, we sat for a long while without saying anything. Mother stared out the window. When the intensity of the situation had subsided, Mother and I talked more calmly. She turned from the window, smiled, and asked, "Where is your dad today?"

I looked at her and, mustering the kindest voice I could, told her, "Mother, you know Dad died about 20 years ago."

"Oh yes, I remember that. I don't know why I ask those things."

It was not a good day for her. I thought I noticed a little slurring of words, maybe the effect of the medicine. We continued to sit there, saying nothing.

Mother broke the silence. "Did you enjoy the lunch I fixed today?" she asked, before acknowledging that she did not have a kitchen and did not cook anymore. Finally, Mother asked if my wife was okay, showing she still knew family. Mother seemed to move in and out of reality.

Mother admitted that she felt low at times. She knew our conversation had not gone well that day, but she did not remember any details. She took it upon herself to be the cause of the problem. Before the visit was over, we discussed her money and the fact that the room was what she needed now. While she acknowledged this to be true, it did not make life easier for her that day. As I was leaving, she held onto me and kissed me several times.

The next day, Mother went on a heavier dose of medication. The neurologist increased her anti-anxiety medication to three times a day and added the mood stabilizer Depakote.

The weekend staff had reported that Mother was particularly anxious on weekends, but the weekday staff indicated that the anxiety was an everyday occurrence.

With Friends Like These …

As soon as Mother moved into Memory Care, she was paired with ML, another resident who had also made the move from Personal Care. ML was from Texas, was Baptist, and according to the staff was "direct." Remembering me from previous visits, ML called me over to ask why we had stuck Mother with her. Part of ML's complaint was that Mother talked constantly about her three sons, leading ML to tell Mother that if she heard any more about them "she would go crazy!" Mother responded that if ML wasn't so mean, she would have more friends.

Worsening Mind

After six weeks I realized I was not cringing every time the phone rang. After Mother's foiled attempt at packing up and going home, I had resolved (again) to not get angry with her. Unfortunately, she had not made a similar resolution because she did not remember there was any earlier anger.

My wife and I went for a visit and were met with a greeting from one of the staff, "She is going to be so happy so see you!"

"And you and the others are too," I responded. She smiled knowingly, and I knew that Mother had been at it again. The staff member went to Mother and told her, "Look who I found." Mother almost ran to us, crying and saying how glad she was that we had come.

"The Lord just sent you here today," Mother said.

When we entered her room Mother asked, "Where is your dad? I haven't seen him lately." I paused, looked at her and said, "Mother, you know Dad died 20 years ago."

Quickly, and almost with embarrassment, Mother replied, "I knew that. I don't know why I say those things. But he has been so real to me today." As we moved further into the room, she turned to me and asked again, "Where is your dad?" The rest of the visit was spent reminding Mother that this was her room and she did not have to move.

Mother jumped at my invitation to walk outside. It was the slowest I had ever seen her move with her walker. I held her arm the whole time, and she seemed to veer to one side a lot. She could make the walk back to her room but was exhausted.

As we were preparing to leave, Mother thanked us for coming and gave us several kisses. She was calmer after we left than before we got there, but she seemed less collected than usual Later, I found out that Mother had called a brother on Sunday evening to ask when we were all coming to stay in the room across the hall. She had also fallen that night while trying to sit on her walker.

I saw a noticeable decline in Mother that week. I looked back at notes I had made on a television documentary based on David Shenk's book, *The Forgetting: A Portrait of Alzheimer's*.[1] All the doctors interviewed spoke of Alzheimer's patients as being difficult to characterize because of their individual differences. However, there were certain patterns to their behavior: 1) the world goes backward, 2) there is denial that anything is wrong, and 3) along with the loss of memory comes a loss of self and lack of recognition of self. Along with *pretending* to know what he or she is doing, the Alzheimer's sufferer loses all sense of who they are as a person. Mother certainly had some of these traits.

"I Didn't Know How It Would Be"

I will admit to dreading the visit with Mother that Sunday afternoon. I had heard that she had been so obsessed and persistent about "finding her family" that she was beginning to bother the other residents. A change in her anti-anxiety medication was ordered, and Mother had been on this new regimen for a few days before I visited. As we walked to her room, Mother announced, "I didn't know how it would be today." I was unsure of what she meant.

She was pleased that I had come over, of course, and seemed to be in a relaxed mood. After her usual questions, Mother added, "Is this the place I will live until I die?"

I was not ready to address such a blunt question, so I reminded her that this was her home.

"I feel like I have been through a narrow tunnel, then it widened, and then it got narrow again," she said. "Have you ever had that feeling?"

I confessed that I had not, and thought for sure that the Xanax was having an effect.

"Do you think I died and came back?" she asked. Mother talked more about death this day than any other. It was on her mind. "I never thought I would be in this condition. I did not know how it would be." After so many years trying to get back to normal, Mother finally seemed to be accepting that her mind was failing.

"I did not know my mind was this bad. Did you?" she asked at one point.

I said that I had known.

"How long have I been like this?"

I told her about eight months, and she seemed to accept it. More than once, she admitted that she could not trust her mind anymore.

During our drive into the countryside that afternoon, Mother asked how Dad was. I hesitated a moment, and then said as kindly as I could that Dad had been dead for about 20 years.

"Oh yes. I knew that," Mother said without passion.

I explained: "Mother, Dad was very sick for the last few years. It was okay for him to go."

Mother agreed, knowing that better than any of us since she had been Dad's nursemaid for many years.

"I did not know how it would be," she said contemplatively. "I did not know how it would be."

Maybe this statement betrayed some thought about her last years on this earth. She seemed to be calm—almost at peace.

Realization? Not Really

The "better" times faded as the days wore on. Mother seemed to retain the fact that her mental condition was not good, and she kept referring to herself as being "crazy." Despite her realization, there were times she still thought she was just visiting the motel or hospital and would be going home soon.

About two months into Memory Care, a big step backward occurred. When I arrived for a mid-week visit, Mother was playing a game. A staff member let me in and hugged me, a sign that things had been rough. She related how Mother had been going on about her sons and visits so much that she almost called me. The staff member had been given extra medication to help calm Mother at night but had not wanted to give it to her—why, I did not know; it was the only thing keeping all of us sane. I was invited to go and surprise Mother with my visit.

"Did you come to take me home?" Mother began.

As always, I replied: "Mother, this *is* home. *This* is your home." As many times as I had seen Mother's mind fail her, I was still surprised at how little information she retained.

Mother then asked how long she had been like "this." I told her two years.

"Two years?" she repeated with surprise.

For Mother, a whole block of time was missing.

Anticipating her next question, I added: "Mother, during this time you have acted with kindness to everyone and have been yourself. You just do not remember." While she found some relief in my comment, she was more focused on how unbelievable all of this—her life and situation—was.

"I cannot believe this," she crooned. "Not that I doubt your word, but it seems so unreal."

As we waded through the conversation, I pushed her toward another subject. "Let's not continue to talk about the same thing. Let's talk about something else. What did you do today?"

The problem was that she did not remember what she had done, so she spoke in generalities, and soon we returned to the same conversations as always: about Mother, her home, where everyone else was, whether her money was holding out, and where Dad was.

I realized, at last, that there was nothing else we could talk about. Mother was unable to reason anymore, and for her there was no other conversation to be had other than about herself. Mother said she had thought Audie was with her. I asked if she felt as if Audie was with her at times, or did she remember later that Audie *had* been with her. Although my question was unclear, it seemed the feeling was the latter.

Your Dad

Mother's anti-anxiety medication seemed to be working as intended. She would still interrogate the staff about when her sons would visit, but the questioning was less intense, and Mother could be distracted for a while with other activities. She seemed to feel better and less anxious, but something else was bothering her: She was ready to go home!

Mother and Dad in the front yard of their home.

Home was ill-defined, changing from place to place. I replayed the scenario once again of why she had sold her home and moved to be close to me. It was clear that Mother remembered something of the past, namely how much she loved home and doing for everyone. Going home meant going to be with family. Mother then began to ask about Dad. He was her first love—a true love never forgotten—although now it seemed as though she asked about him without any real emotion or feeling. He was simply another person in the family.

"How is *your* dad?" Mother had often asked me more recently.

Sometimes, she used his first name. To the news that he had died, she said nothing or "Oh yes, I knew that."

On one occasion she singled him out for going to the movies. "He is going to stop that," Mother emphasized. Mother did not like the movies and recalled the time that she had been stranded with two small children—my older brothers—at a showing of *Abbot and Costello Meet Frankenstein* while Dad attended a civic meeting. Her admonition that Dad was going to stop going to the movies was emotional.

"I Messed Up" or "Dan Is Messed Up"

On a Sunday visit in May, about three months into Memory Care, Mother was sitting on her walker seat in the nurses' office looking at the monitor for the door and waiting for me to arrive. Even so, she seemed surprised to see me. She asked if there was some place we could go and talk; she had forgotten she had a room.

"I messed up. I just messed up today," she lamented.

"Why did you mess up?" I asked, lightheartedly.

"I haven't planned my day. I am just lazy and did not do anything."

The best explanation was that Mother still remembered what she used to do, or what she supposed she was to do, but could no longer do it. She was frustrated, and in her mind was a laggard. She saw the staff working and thought she should be working too. She felt useless.

I began to see signs of giving up. Mother moved slowly—possibly because of recent falls—and there was definite mental impairment. After three months in Memory Care, Mother's health had declined significantly. She was anxious at times and would browbeat the staff to call one of her sons just to hear our voices and to know that we knew where she was. There was also no real conversation with Mother anymore, but instead a one-way discussion of the issue of the day.

Mother's "messing up" was the theme for a while—with one variation: As we were leaving to see the doctor, Mother turned the tables and announced, "Dan is messed up, and I have got to get him straightened out." While I *was* transitioning along with Mother, I did not think I had come that far!

The "messing up" Mother mostly focused on was related to her falls. Mother never liked to be the center of attention, especially if it meant creating a spectacle such as falling in public. The falls created a lot of excitement for the staff as well as for Mother. After three falls, she was lucky that she had not broken any bones—perhaps the Evista she had taken to ward off bone loss had paid off.

At least two of the falls were the result of the walker getting away from Mother when she tried to sit on it because she could not remember to lock the wheels. The days of Mother using her walker were coming to an end. Her trusty companion, the one she had chosen to be like the other ladies in independent living, was retired for Mother's safety and replaced with a lightweight walker she had to lift and move. She was not happy about this.

Mind Medicines—Starting from Scratch

Mother's treatment with Depakote and Xanax to control her anxiety was initially effective. The Depakote was administered twice a day, and the Xanax was given as needed to control fits of anxiety. Mother seemed better and more positive. Her status, however, had changed dramatically in the three months she had been in Memory Care. The nurse explained the change as a reversal back to Mother's condition before any medication was given. Xanax was reported to have this effect.

Even though Mother was sleepy most all the time and her speech was sometimes slurred, her anxiety was no longer under control. The neurologist was concerned that the Depakote might be the culprit and stopped both the Depakote and the Xanax, replacing them with Seroquel and Lexapro. Finding the right medication for Mother's illness was difficult. In addition to having extreme fits of anxiety, Mother also fell four times in one week.

I visited Mother during this period of medication change, and it was soon obvious that the new medication had not kicked in—she did not recognize me at first, calling me by my brother's name. Mother insisted on a conference with me and the head nurse to discuss her "messing up."

Several attempts to dissuade her did not work. She was insistent that the staff knew she was "acting crazy" and messing up. She *needed* to inform them. Mother started to want things done for her, things she once would have done for herself. It was as though she did not trust herself to do them. At one point, she asked, "Would you put my toothpaste on my brush?"

"I will, Mother, but do the ladies do this for you?" I asked as I squeezed out the paste.

"Who bought the little house?" Mother asked, as she cleaned her teeth.

All I could think she meant was her and Dad's first residence, a little house just across the highway from her parents. Her mother lived close by, half-a-stone's throw away, and no doubt it was a great comfort when Mother began housekeeping for the first time and when the first baby arrived. The time would have been about 1938. Then she asked about Dad and where he was and if he was coming by. There was no easing her fears.

As I prepared to leave, Mother said she did not want me to go. I told her I had errands to run. Mother quietly told me she knew I did, *and* still did not want me to go.

"I cannot make it if you leave me," she pleaded, pulling a big guilt trip.

She questioned who would take care of her and what would she do. Her mind seemed totally blank. I finally pulled myself together and left, feeling bad about both our situations.

It reminded me of the head nurse's recent comment: "I have never seen anyone so caught up with family. Your mother's adjustment is taking a long time."

I know, I thought. I know.

I wondered if Mother would ever adjust. It seemed as if all of us—Mother, the staff, and me—were frustrated, and two of us (me and the staff) were anxiously waiting for the new medication to kick in.

Messing Up (Again), But in a Different Way

It was clear that Mother did not like to mess up, which she lamented for days. On my Sunday visit, I ushered Mother to her room so we could talk. A brother had received a call from Mother the night before where she "confessed" she had messed up and instructed him to take her home.

"I've messed up," Mother repeated to me in her room.

I felt like bantering with her a bit and asked, "How have you messed up, Mother?"

"I have not been honest," she replied.

She caught me off guard. I do not recall that she used the word "lied" but instead claimed to have "exaggerated."

"About what?" I asked, wondering what skeletons might fall out of the closet today.

"Well, I haven't been honest with things, and it messes people up."

"Who has been messed up?"

"I exaggerated and was not truthful."

The conversation was going nowhere. I finally told her that letting the subject drop was probably best because everything had been resolved and everyone was okay. She agreed, adding again that only she was to blame and would suffer. Was Mother going over real regrets, or were these just the feelings of someone with Alzheimer's?

I changed the subject to a favorable topic: food. "What did you have for lunch?" I began.

As our conversation focused on food, Mother made another surprising comment. "Maybe you can just dip some vegetables from the pot for your supper."

I repeated that the staff would cook supper there, but the conversation quickly turned upside down. She began to talk about "Dan" as if I were another person and not the one in front of her. I was not sure if Mother was confusing names or did not realize I was there.

"Dan went over to see Mother (meaning her own mother), and they went over to see Dan's mother. They had dinner with my brother and sister-in-law." All of these people, except Dan of course, are long deceased. During the ramblings, Mother often referred to "our children," making me wonder if she thought I was Dad. I played along and did not tell her that I was Dan.

The rest of our conversations that day made no sense either, and many subjects were dropped without any understanding, resolution, or conclusion. As I prepared to leave, I asked one of the workers about any happenings that day that might have caused issues. The worker responded, "She has just been telling me today that she messed up." The nurse said that they had given Mother additional Seroquel at 11 o'clock that morning, but nothing was working. Mother was still agitated and talking about going home. The nurse repeated that both doctors thought Mother's condition was worsening. Mother's "I messed up" slogan continued into early June.

On my next visit, I tried to usher Mother and her walker back to her room, but she balked and said with insistence, "I do not need to go in there. I need to go home." I gently maneuvered her into her room and said kindly that this *was* her home. She looked confused and said in a slightly belligerent voice, "Dan, you do not understand what is happening."

No truer words had ever been spoken. I was confounded by Mother's comments about honesty as well as her mixing up family members. And it was never clear to me if Mother had a basis for real regrets, untruths, and dishonesty, or if it was all made up.

The Clinic

On the day I left town for two weeks, Mother had a major meltdown, which I found out about late in the day after a phone call from my oldest brother. He said not to come home, that he would take care of the situation, which was a doozie.

Mother had shown signs of agitation and been repeating the confusing theme of her "dishonesty" for some time. She still wanted to go back home to her mother. On this beautiful June day, she would not be settled; she roamed the floor for hours, asking everyone in sight if they had a car and would take her home. She had packed her clothes to leave before telling a staff member she felt as though she would die.

The woman replied casually, "Naw, you're not gonna die."

"Then, I will kill myself!" Mother insisted.

There were three things that could get a resident kicked out of Memory Care: the inability to carry out basic functions, threatening the staff, and contemplating suicide. My brother took Mother immediately to a special clinic where they treated psychiatric disorders. A psychiatrist evaluated Mother and worked through her medications, discarding old ones, prescribing new ones, and adjusting them for dosage, time of day, and other situations. The psychiatrist watched her for 48 hours, and Mother began to improve within a few days.

In late June, Mother was released from the clinic and allowed to return to Memory Care with a new set of prescriptions.

Post-Clinic

I visited Mother two days after her return. I was dreading this visit but was pleasantly surprised, however, by her contentment. In fact, Mother and I both used the word *contentment* a lot to describe her feeling. I reported to my brothers that things were looking up.

Mother was talkative. In fact, she talked louder than normal, and I wondered if her hearing was worse. I did not know how this visit would go. What would we talk about? As it turned out, Mother led the way; however, the conversation wandered all over the place. Part of this wandering stemmed from me trying to find a topic of interest while assessing Mother's mental status. The other part of the wandering was that Mother was sometimes here and sometimes back where she grew up.

Mother did not mind my asking her questions such as what year she thought it was and seemed to take in stride that her mental facilities were failing. We talked about her being 92 years old. She remembered her birthday, but then she wandered off a bit, thinking a sister had been born on her birthday. As we followed this trail and I reminded her of her birthday again, Mother commented: "Well, they go together, don't they? Sort of go over to the next year."

When she would wrap herself up in a sentence and get lost, Mother would say, "It just sort of moves around and takes care of itself." For example, on planting the crops (back home), she offered, "The crops just seem to come up each year"—as if by themselves because the other part of the process, the planting, she did not remember. It seemed as if she brought verbal order to these situations and then everything was fine.

Before I left, ML came by. To my surprise, Mother smiled, greeted ML, and asked her to come in. (I guessed they were friends again.) The head nurse had recently told me: "You know, we separated your mother and ML because of all the fussing. But no sooner had that been done, your mother picked up her placemat and silverware and moved back to the same table—with ML."

ML and I exchanged pleasantries, and then she said to Mother, "If you are coming to dinner, you might plan to stay a while. We have lots of forms to fill out." This comment led to a very confusing conversation for all concerned.

Mother looked at ML with surprise and asked, "What?"

"Forms. Forms!" ML repeated.

The quizzical look on Mother's face indicated either that she did not hear ML or that she did not understand what she meant. I tried to add some clarity.

I said to ML, "I will get mother to supper and then leave for the evening." I repeated this sentence to Mother.

Mother then said to ML, "Should I go with you and Dan to her house?"

ML was then the one with the quizzical look and said to Mother, "I do not understand," to which Mother replied, "I thought we were all going to Mother's for supper."

I do not recall exactly how we ended this conversation, but supper time rolled around, and Mother and I walked to the dining room. As we walked, Mother asked, "How do I get to the dining room?"

Our Conversations Are Different Now

Mother was so happy to see me and my wife on a Sunday visit in July. She was sitting in the dining room having a snack when we arrived. As we walked back to her room, I had to guide Mother almost every step to keep her from veering off in one direction or another until we reached her door. It was not clear she knew her room.

I thought about the conversations I had been having with Mother. At times, her pontifications were generalized and based on her way of living, but at other times our conversations consisted of nothing but questions from Mother on the doings of her siblings and others, mostly those no longer living. I started to "play games" with Mother and not answer her questions directly. I did not try to lie to her or trick her; instead, I simply went along with the "thoughts at hand." For example, Mother asked, "Did Lilly begin some new adventure or change in her job?" To which I replied, "No, everything is about the same." I did not say Aunt Lilly had died six years ago.

I said similar things about Aunt Audie, Uncle Aubrie, Aunt Bernice, and Aunt Mildred. I tried to play off as much as possible without correcting Mother, explaining to her how it really was, or telling her that someone was dead. After all, the same question would come up again later. My conversations with Mother had become a monumental change for us.

Sometimes Mother would ask a question about one of her siblings, which I tried to avoid, as I steered the conversation toward growing up on the farm or gardening. Sometimes she interjected questions out of the blue such as, "Did I ever live in Ohio?" or declared, "I felt like I went out west for a few days." More often than not, the conversations took on a disorganized tone.

At one point Mother stated that "Dan really likes to garden." I do not know who she thought she was talking to about Dan. A likely guess would be Uncle Aubrie. He came up again when my brother morphed into Uncle Aubrie. I asked Mother if she remembered when my brother visited Aunt Audie's first-grade class at Rock Ridge School. Mother declared emphatically, "No, he never did that. You see, he had his own way of doing things and went his own way." The way she said it let me know that she was thinking about Uncle Aubrie and not my brother.

Conversations with Mother would likely be different from now on, I suspected. There would be no more exchanging information, asking advice, or even gathering facts on family and places. There was no need any longer to correct Mother's "facts," or try to get her to understand, or tell her that all her family was dead. The idea now was to encourage her to talk about familiar and pleasant things and to maintain her happiness. Who cared if some of her facts were less than accurate? What did it matter if we brothers morphed into Uncle Aubrie and all our spouses were "Winnies"?

Fantasy Validation Therapy

Since it was no longer possible to have coherent conversations with Mother, we played games instead. I received a call from a staff member in late July because Mother wanted to talk to one of her boys, and she was again talking about going home. I hoped we were not going to have to return to the psychiatric clinic. When I arrived at Mother's place, however, I found Mother chatting with her lady friends, just as happy as she could be. As we walked back to Mother's room, the worker asked Mother if she was happy now.

Mother answered, almost with a laugh, "I am always happy. But I am really happy when he comes to see me."

"What did you do today?" I asked to spur the conversation. "Did you have a meeting?"

Mother told me that she had been to a meeting on a previous day and that "they" got things sorted out. She could not remember what things needed sorting but was reassured that "they" were in control. "There was a group that talked about insurance," Mother said. "Did I get a big bill on insurance?" For some reason, insurance was on her mind, but the difficulty came in deciphering if she had actually heard someone there talking about insurance or if, in fact, she was remembering back to when we put her money into an annuity.

"That was all taken care of," I told her to put her mind at ease.

"Good."

My answer seemed to settle *that* issue.

Then I noticed her fingernails. They were a bright red.

"Someone painted your fingernails," I remarked.

"Yes," said Mother with a glint in her eye. "The boys down there painted them."

The boys, I thought. What boys? There were no boys on the staff at that time. Surely, she meant the girls and she was just doing "word play."

"When boys paint your nails, they do a good job," she continued.

"Do you mean *your* boys?" I asked.

"No. The boys down there," she said, pointing in the direction of the staff.

"Are the boys upset by the moves?" she asked, changing direction quickly—and this time meaning *her* boys.

"What moves?"

"Well, all the class changes," Mother continued.

"I think everything went okay and we are fine now."

"Good," said Mother, putting this issue to rest as well.

It was time to go. Mother's supper was about to be served, so I walked her down to the dining area. She thanked me for coming and happily turned to take her seat. While I had concluded that these types of conversations were now the way forward, I had that idea confirmed at a monthly support group meeting of family members of Memory Care residents. Everyone there said that the best way to proceed was to just go along with the loved one because the next moment would be a new subject with the old one forgotten. Chaplain Mark called this "fantasy validation therapy." It seemed my method actually had a name.

Starvation and Normal

Gina, the social director, was technically and financially responsible for the Memory Care operation, but she was also the residents' confidant, supporter, and best listener. Gina related with gusto her conversations with Mother. After Mother returned from the psychiatric clinic, her appetite grew enormously—she was eating "everything in sight," according to Gina. Mother could not be sated. She ate Jello, cookies, candy bars—you name it. While her eating habits were surprising in themselves, even more surprising was her lack of remembering any of it.

As Mother and I sat and talked in the activities room one day, she told me, within earshot of Gina, that she did not have much of an appetite. Gina laughed out loud. Mother repeated this comment frequently, likely "willing it to be." It was untrue, and Gina reminded us at our support group meetings that 'normal is a setting on the washing machine."

What's in a Name?

Mother's new medication regime seemed to hold out through the summer. I continued to visit on Wednesdays and Sundays just before her dinner. Our visits now were pleasant and cordial, but I began to notice that Mother asked a lot about a fellow named Dan.

"Have you seen Dan yet?" she would ask. "He wants to see you."

This confusion happened several times, and I asked "Mother, do you know who I am?"

She looked at me coyly and smiled. "You are Dan," she said calmly but with authority.

"It seems as if you get me confused at times."

"I just get names mixed up," Mother explained.

Maybe so, but it was happening very often. Sometimes she did confuse names, but this was different. At times she would call me Dan, but at other times, while I was someone familiar to her, I was not Dan. "Not-me Dan" seemed to come by often. He talked to Mother and told her what he liked to do. Mother said that she really wanted me to meet this fellow. One day she was telling "Not-me Dan" about Dan and his love of gardening, and another time

Mother told me that Dan had come by but that she had not seen him because she was talking with Audie.

On the day that Mother asked me who was standing in front of her and if I had seen Dan, I practiced fantasy validation therapy and answered, "No, I did not see him today, but I will see him sometime." Mother seemed to be okay with that because she really wanted Dan and "Not-me-Dan" to meet. It was never clear during these times who *I* was, but if I asked, "Mother, who am I?" she would immediately say my name and confirm that she knew me. Most of the time, Mother could name all three of her sons, but at times, she could not. I suspected that she was beginning to forget me, and maybe all of us.

Mother Always

As we sat and visited in Mother's room, she looked at her newspaper and actually read some of the front page. As she read, I thought I would close my eyes—not sleep mind you, but just briefly rest. When I opened one eye, Mother was fumbling around in her drawer. I knew what she was doing. But I asked anyway, "Mother, what are you looking for?"

She did not give me a clear answer. Instead, she got up out of her chair a second time and fumbled again, this time finding something that would work. She placed a shirt over my bare arms as I reclined in the big chair. "I did not want you to be cold," she gently said.

I said I would check to see if there were any event going on in the activities room. Mother agreed that was a good idea and asked me to go and check it out and let her know. I got up from the chair and began to walk out. "Hold your shoulders up," she ordered. Being a mother is a full-time job—always.

Lucidity

"I was so hungry," Mother volunteered. "They said they did not have anything to eat before supper, but I showed them," Mother said with the defiant flair of her old self. Her comments foreshadowed the rest of the day.

"I want to trim your toenails today," I said.

"Oh, that would be wonderful," Mother said, returning to a kinder attitude. "I will be glad when I can do that again myself."

"I know," I replied, using fantasy validation therapy, "but for now I will help out."

Mother had on pantyhose, which she claimed were knee socks, and it took a little effort on both our parts to free her feet. I had brought with me a pair of toenail clippers. As I lifted her swollen feet, I noticed that some of the toenails were digging into the skin.

"I used to have a small pair of scissors to trim my nails," Mother said, "but someone stole them." Part of my enlightenment on this visit was that Mother did sometimes remember things correctly: She had, in fact, had a small pair of scissors stolen by someone—me. I had found those small, pointed scissors soon after she moved, so I had promptly taken them away.

I did not want her to cut herself. As I trimmed her toenails, Mother was intently involved with every snip, pulling some soft nail fragments away in the process.

After we finished, I helped her to re-dress in socks instead of pantyhose, and continued to talk. As she pulled on her socks, Mother said angrily, "Someone has stolen my clothes! I used to have a ton of everyday clothes."

She was right again. She indeed did have more pants, tops, socks, and shoes—and again I had stolen them.

"Mother," I said as gently as I could, "I have your clothes at home. You did not have enough room, so I took some home to keep. No one has stolen anything." In fact, not only had I "stolen" her clothes, but I had also lied to her: I had given away most of them and thrown away the ones that were ragged.

Mother also told me she had been working pretty hard that day. As she talked, it became clear that Mother considered her games and supervised coloring as her work. It *was* like work. She didn't always like to do it, and she tired of it, but these tasks were what she was given to do. She was right that they were her job.

Finally, she asked me, "How are your parents?" This unusual question did not throw me. I knew Mother did not mean my parents, but instead my family and children. "Word play" had occurred, and she had simply used the wrong word. Knowing this, I no longer thought that Mother was out of it or did not know who I was. In fact, she was very much with it today.

Before I left, I checked to make sure she had all her toiletries. I cleaned her glasses and walked her down to the dining room. She was still hungry and never once told me she could not eat a thing. Her tablemate greeted her, and I left. Today's visit had been something of another epiphany for me. Yes, Mother was confused, but she also had some things right, if not completely accurate: things stolen, her job, my parents. It seemed I had gained a bit of lucidity into Mother's world.

Tugging at My Heart

On a late October visit, Mother had been crying. She said she needed to go home because that was where all the family was.

"Did you come to take me home?" she asked.

I tried to practice fantasy validation therapy by telling her that her home looked very good, attempting to avoid a direct answer—but it did not work this time.

"I have *another* home," Mother said pointedly. "Do Aubrie and Winnie live here too?"

I told her that Aubrie and Winnie did not live where she did and left it at that. I tried to move on to another subject, but Mother was having none of it. I was being sucked into a big swirl of mental chaos—thoughts about home and going back or maybe just getting out of where she was. As we sat down to talk, Mother kept up her assault on her current home.

"Maybe we should just buy a home and then you boys could have it after I am not here." she said.

"We've done that before," I replied, but my point was lost. "You have help here. Folks here help you with your medicine, washing, and meals."

Mother just looked at me. She made a comment on renting that I did not follow. To me, it seemed as though she wanted to avoid a fight, but she did not buy what I was selling that day. After another comment on Aubrie and Winnie, Mother began to ask about who (in her family) was around or had visited.

"I think Dan and his wife stayed with me last night," Mother said rather positively. Then, backing off a bit she added, "Didn't they?"

"No. I don't think so," I replied. Then I asked, "Mother, do you know who I am?"

"Yes, you are Danny. My last to be born," Mother added to reinforce that she knew who I was.

My visit that day was not as good as other recent ones. Mother seemed to be thinking about something else as I talked endlessly, trying to make the visit work. She listened, often not knowing what I said, until her eyes became heavy.

"Are you getting sleepy?" I asked, hoping she would not fall asleep during one of my interesting stories about my garden.

"No. I'm not sleepy," Mother said sweetly.

This visit with Mother was my first since the psychiatrist had added Trazadone to her list of daily prescriptions. The Atavan seemed to be less effective in reducing Mother's anxiety, so we hoped this new medication would work better. She seemed calm and relaxed, but at the same time was hell-bent on going home.

That night, when I revisited the day with Mother, I felt very bad that she seemed to really want to leave and go home. I wondered again if we had done the right thing by her, but I *knew* we had done the right thing—the only thing we could do. She was in the right place for her, but her desires still tugged at my heart.

Birthday Number 93

As January 29th approached, we asked Mother if she remembered her birthday. She said she did—I do not think she ever missed it. The first big decision we had to make was whether to take Mother to my house to celebrate. Discussing this with nurses and others, we decided the best plan was to have the party at Mother's place. That way she would not be traumatized by a new environment, and the other residents would have a party too. I remembered the neurologist's warning on routine and familiarity.

We brothers and our wives made plans to meet at Mother's apartment on Sunday. The staff in Memory Care could not have been more accommodating. They helped with set up, made coffee, watched the cake to make sure no one "got into it," and seated the residents at their places. The cake shop had piped "Happy Birthday, Mother" in red letters and red roses on the top of a chocolate cake. We put the cake and balloons at Mother's seat—but we forgot the candles.

As Mother was escorted to her place, she smiled and talked and had, apparently, looked forward to her birthday party. Mother had a hard time seeing her piece of cake on her plate, so I cut the cake and fed her bites. I was too slow, so she would also cut bites. She quickly finished the entire piece of cake. As we opened gifts and read cards, Mother had another piece of cake. It was not clear if she did not remember eating, did not know she was full—or just loved chocolate cake!

Mother, although excited about her birthday, wanted us to get Dad because he "needed to be there." (Although Dad seemed to have been forgotten for a long while earlier, that first love seemed to have returned, and she had mentioned him often of late.) I told her, without fantasy validation therapy, that Dad was dead. She had a strange reaction, and not the usual, "Oh yes, I knew that." It was more like she did not know it. Mother enjoyed the two hours or so, but soon forgot about her birthday party.

"Am I in an Institution?"

As Mother and I talked during one of my weekday visits, the door to the apartment suddenly opened. A newcomer by the name of Jane walked directly into Mother's room. Jane had a stare that was unsettling. She did not talk and looked straight ahead and stared. She always held a pillow close to her chest.

Jane stood in front of me and stared. I spoke to her, then quickly left to get help from the staff. A worker came and escorted Jane out of the room. She went peaceably, leaving Mother and me alone. Unlike Mother, Jane *looked* like someone who should be in a dementia unit. "She just wanders around," Mother said in a complaining way. Then she looked at me and asked, "Am I in an institution?"

I wondered what Mother was thinking and what she meant. We have all seen unpleasant images of mental institutions, with their screaming patients, scurrying nurses and staff, and general confusion. Mother's residence was nothing like that—it was a good place. But Mother *was* in an institution, and I think she knew it all along. Maybe Jane convinced her.

My Long-Lost Sister?

Gina often mentioned Mother's strong need for companionship, and much of this companionship fell upon Gina. Mother took up an awful lot of Gina's time, and she looked for other ways for Mother to have personal interactions. Young interns and volunteers gave time at the retirement center, and when a volunteer showed up, the director knew what to do. At one point, Gina was able to have someone visit with Mother every day.

Some of the women in independent living, where Mother had started her new life, volunteered to visit. One, however, seemed to be a special case. B lived in the community and had a mother with Alzheimer's who had died a while back. B said Mother reminded her of her own mother. B would visit one or two times a week. She seemed to enjoy visits with Mother.

When I arrived for a Thursday visit in February, Mother was in the activities room looking at dog pictures with B. Mother called me by my brother's name. I corrected her, joking with her and B that I was much better looking than him. Mother laughed and said how good-looking we both were. B told Mother she could now go and visit with her son. For the first time, Mother seemed hesitant to leave. Mother turned to B and asked, "Do you want to come with us?"

B declined, probably happy for a break. I was surprised that Mother would want to bring B along. I think Mother was the most contented I had seen her since her admission to Memory Care. She was willing to accept B into her inner circle—the only time I recalled this happening. We often said that it was Mother's own fault that she had only sons and no daughters to care for her. Was B my long-lost sister? Maybe, today she was.

Twisted Up With Real Things

James VanOosting, the author of "The Last Bursts of Memory" in *The American Scholar*,[2] wrote about the confusion in his father and his vivid but inaccurate stories. VanOosting summarized several observations, noticeably that: dementia causes misconceptions of time, stories get confused, collages emerge from the mix-and-match of free-flowing memory, and stories are created. Further, VanOosting noted that the more important the memory, the more likely it is that our brains will revise it, embellishing or downplaying parts.

At times Mother showed characteristics similar to those seen in VanOosting's assessment of his father. In Mother, however, it expressed itself in her constant yearning for home. It seemed as if home was a concept rather than a real place. I wondered if she could describe *home* at all now.

"Mother," I asked, "where is home to you?"

"I don't know," she replied, adding, "I know this is home. Has Mother just gone away for a while?"

"You know, Mother, that your mother is dead. She died 60 years ago."

Mother's expression did not change. She just looked at me with the same expression, then said, "Sometimes my mind get twisted up with the real things." It could not have been expressed any better. There was some reality mixed in with the unreal. Mother could never be sure which was real and which was unreal.

Only Two Things Guaranteed: This Time, Taxes

Even if you are 93 and blind in one eye, you must file your taxes. I wondered what a person did if they were in a dementia unit and did not have anyone to file their taxes for them. Luckily for Mother, she had a son.

Working up the forms was no issue, and Mother owed nothing. There was a concern, however, about how to sign the forms. I feared that Mother could not sign her name any longer. She had not needed to do that in a while, and I was worried that she would not be able to do it now. I brought three copies of the signature pages for each of the federal and state tax returns so she could practice her signature. Mother was kind and calm during our practice.

Her first try on the federal taxes was pretty good. The letters rose a bit and were not on the line—but were good enough for government work. Mother's legibility, however, decreased with each subsequent attempt on the state form. She seemed to get confused, even on the letters of her name. She had written those letters so effortlessly on the federal form. Perhaps it was frustration or tiredness, but she seemed to struggle. The first attempt on the state taxes was passable, although the middle initial was below the line. I thought she could do better. The second attempt was a disaster, and she did not even finish the signature. Mother seemed to lose the knowledge of which letters to write. We tried one final time: This signature was her best. Mother's taxes were easy; her signature was hard.

All Still Kids and in the Big House

I could always tell when Mother was driving the staff nuts. It was apparent as soon as they let me in and said, "You came just at the right time!"

As it turned out, I was late on this April Wednesday. I should have visited the previous day. For two days Mother had been anxious and badgered the staff about her brothers, sisters, family, and when she would be going home. A nurse was trying to get her to take her anti-anxiety pill when I arrived. Mother was stooped and red-eyed. Her face was drawn. She was in a bad way.

"Hi, Mother," I said with a lilt in my voice. "How are you today?"

Mother looked at me and said, "I am so glad to see you."

We walked back to her room. She was unsteady. As we reached her room, I asked her if she was not feeling well because the nurse had mentioned a doctor's appointment. When I brought this up, I caused Mother even more anxiety, and she became worried that she had forgotten something. The only thing she was *not* concerned about was seeing a doctor because she was sick.

It was possible that someone had told Mother she had a doctor's appointment on Monday. Whatever the case, it was impossible today to get a rational response out of her.

"Audie put me in my bed last night, you know. She got me up today," Mother allowed.

"Have you been thinking a lot about Audie lately?"

This phrase was my way of telling Mother that what she said was not reality, but I am not sure that she picked up on the comment.

"Do you think about your growing up a lot?" I continued.

"Not a lot," Mother replied.

She might not think about it, but she sure talked about it! Mother kept going back to the house, the big house, the house her dad had built. Her thoughts flickered between being there and looking back at events that had occurred there. I could never be sure where she was. The entire visit was an array of discontinuous, rambling comments.

"Do you live in the big house?" she suddenly asked.

"What house do you mean, Mother?"

"The one where all the others live," she said, obviously referring to her home place.

"No," I said. "I live in another house."

"Where is your house?"

Somewhere in our rambling conversation that day, Mother mentioned that all the property deeds were put together, which was true. Granddad Duncan had several fields that he farmed, and Mother commented that her father had not sold the place, but that it was still in the family. That was also true. Uncle Gene had bought it from the other family members and lived there after he retired from the U.S. Army. His children still own it. Mother talked about Gene and Bea as if they still lived in the big house, as they indeed had for some years.

"You could have lots of apartments, or even a cotton gin," Mother suggested. Likely, she did not mean cotton gin, but that was the word that came out. Mother's comment best summed up her mind that day: "I wish we were all still kids."

Never Failing to Amaze

It was time to see the eye doctor again. During the previous appointment, Mother had not been able to see the mirror for reflecting letters and numbers. She did not score well.

Mother, however, never failed to amaze. This time she was alert, could see the mirror, seemed to hear and understand the eye doctor, and performed quite well. The best news was that her eyes were as good, or slightly better, than they had been the last time. Eye pressures were very good, and while there was some deterioration in her "good" eye, it was holding up pretty well, and there was nothing to do now. Even her eyeglass prescription was correct.

As Mother and I walked back into her room, she told me that my brother had been over and had brought his baby, and the baby had cried a lot. I passed this comment off, putting it into the same bin as the questions about Mildred and Audie. Later, my brother sent an email. He wrote: "I dropped by to see Mother today while visiting and supposedly helping my daughter. Unfortunately, I had a grandchild with me who suddenly realized that 'mommy' was not close by. After I took her outside for a half hour or so while she cried inconsolably, she finally calmed down and we visited with Mother for about 30 minutes."

So, Mother had it mostly right. My brother had been there, he had a baby, and the baby cried a lot. Mother's comments brought up a lingering question: What does she remember? I was never sure.

What Makes a Support Group?

The Memory Care support group met monthly, and all those who met felt its importance. We talked about the issues of the afflicted and those of the caregivers. The afflicted might not know their children, but they liked them. One person in the support group talked about a relative who had dementia so severely that she did not recognize her own son. The afflicted mother asked one day, "Who was that *kind* man?" The mother could not recognize her son, but she recognized kindness.

Folks in the support group mentioned changes in their afflicted relatives. Sundowners Syndrome seemed to be common; going into the rooms of other residents was a problem; wandering was new to some. Then the discussion turned to the caregivers. One of the major characteristics of this group was *denial*. Folks just could not believe their parent had dementia. Another common characteristic of attendees was guilt. What do you do to help? How long do you stay for a visit? How often do you visit? I could relate to all of it.

Mother, the Good Employee

On a Friday in early July, Mother's demeanor reminded me of her earlier years of concentrating and working hard at her job. Her current job comprised tasks the staff gave the residents to do to keep them busy. For Mother, separating straws by color was her job that day.

I sat awhile and watched as Mother worked. After a moment she noticed I was there and was glad to see me. I waited for her to finish separating the straws in her hand. When she finished, I asked her if she wanted to visit in her room.

"Well, there are lot more straws," she responded. "People have to eat."

"They will hold," I said. "People can use them as they are."

Mother was okay to leave the straws then, but I found it interesting that she still had the old work ethic—she wanted to finish that job.

Old Pictures

I was thinking of a way to make our visits better and more interesting for both Mother and myself. After all, how long can you talk about the weather and how good a day you had? I was tinkering with the idea of bringing some old pictures with me, but I was bothered by this idea, too.

The issue was Mother's incessant focus on family, home, and going back there. Would the pictures help or hurt? I didn't know. Friday had been a good day, one of the few when I wondered (ever so briefly) if she should even be in Memory Care. I had selected several pictures of her sons early in life and a few others to show her.

In her room, I cleaned her glasses and re-tied her shoes. I felt her hands to see how cold they were, and we talked about her hands. It was a time for touch, and Mother seemed to like that. Still not convinced it was a good idea, I pulled out the first picture from the bag. It was a picture of Dad with his three sons. Mother was not in the photo, and we figured she had taken it. She seemed pleased to see it.

"Is that Dan?" Mother asked of the person on the left side.

"No," I said. "I'm the little guy in the middle."

I then pointed out all of her family and remarked that the person on the right was Dad. Mother did not respond. The second photo was a baby picture of her taken in 1919.

"I think that's me," Mother said. "It looks like me."

"That's right," I said, excited that she recognized it.

I then showed Mother a picture of herself standing in the kitchen of our home place when she was about 58 with the fixings of a grand meal all around her. She did not recognize herself or seem to understand the situation. We did not tarry long on this picture.

Next, I showed Mother a picture of all three of her sons with her standing in front of our old home place. She asked if the picture was of her "family," and I told her it was. She could not see very well, and after I told her who was in it, she did not have anything to say, other than she could not see very well. She did not seem to grasp that the picture was of the old home place taken on the day in July when she left her home for good.

The last picture I showed her was a black-and-white photo of Dad's family. Grandmother, who was very elderly, was wrapped in a heavy black coat and standing in front. All of Dad's brothers and their wives were gathered for a grand photo in front of an uncle's brick house. "Is that Dan's dad?" Mother asked.

What an odd way to phrase a question, I thought. Mother did not ask if that was Greshom, but "Is that Dan's dad?" I came around to see the picture better; she had picked out one of Dad's brother who looked just like him. I found Dad and pointed him out. She did not say anything about Dad.

Mother studied the picture, a big, sharp, 8x10 black-and-white photo. Then she began to point out people, but she mixed up Dad's family with hers. I watched her to see if she named any more of her family. She did not and seemed to be through with the picture.

"Did you like seeing the pictures?" I asked. "Would you like for me to bring others?"

"Yes," she said, "I liked seeing them. Bring some more at some time."

There was no resounding call to see more pictures. I was not sure if she enjoyed them or not. Even more, I am not sure what she understood.

Thanksgiving Day and Mother's Family

On Thanksgiving Day, I found Mother in the TV room and huddled in a blanket. We went back to her room to visit. I cleaned her glasses, re-tied her shoes, and felt her hands. These actions were the routine that Mother knew and participated in. Her hands were warm, yet she said how cold it was.

Since the picture-showing of the previous visit seemed to be an okay change in our conversation, I had brought with me a "famous" photo of Mother's whole family that was made back around 1940 in front of her family home. The picture was taken by the big-city newspaper, and the cutline elaborated on the education of Mother's rural family. It was quite a keepsake. I knew Mother had seen it often. I showed her the 5x7 black-and-white photo.

In Mother's family, nephews frequently looked more like their uncles than their fathers. This situation perhaps caused Mother to confuse her older brother with the son from another brother. Mother asked if one of the folks shown was me. I told her no, I had not been born yet. I pointed out each of her brothers and sisters and their spouses.

Mother looked at them and seemed pleased, but there was not much excitement. I pointed out the old family house and the kudzu that Granddad had growing over the front porch every summer. Mother smiled and said she remembered all that. She looked a while at the picture, agreeing with who I said the people were. I asked her if she wanted to keep the picture, but she did not. She said something might happen to it. I said I would keep it at home.

I asked Mother if she remembered a lot about her home and community. She said she did. I asked her, then, if she would like for me to bring a history of it. Mother asked me if it was written by Myric Shaw. While I could not remember the author's name, Mother did! Mother said she would like for me to do that. She then asked, "Is Dan still overseas?"

All I could think was that Mother had looked at a picture of Uncle Gene serving in the army in Europe just after the war. I talked a bit more to keep the conversation going. Mother then asked, "Do your brothers resemble each other?" I think this question again harkened back to a photo and the fact of family resemblance. I responded that I did not think my brothers resembled each other.

Mother closed her eyes and went to sleep. It was time to quit talking and let her rest.

Miss J

Sometime after Mother had entered Memory Care, Miss J became her friend. Miss J had been in Memory Care for a while too. She spoke little, mostly mumbled, and was trying to get records straight—or something like that. Miss J sat at Mother's table for meals, and at times it was only Mother and Miss J. I had begun to make a special effort to speak to Miss J wherever I saw her. To my surprise, she spoke back, softly, but intelligibly. Whenever Mother and Miss J were sitting next to each other when I came to visit, I would take Mother back to her room and leave Miss J, or Miss J would get up and walk away. Miss J respected my time with Mother while still showing an interest in her.

The new head nurse told me that Mother was the dependent one and that Miss J more or less looked after her. Miss J would sit next to Mother and caress her hand. They were always together, often walking. Gina said that Miss J thought Mother was *her* mother and was trying to take care of her and show her where to go. Apparently, this had been Miss J's job before.

I wondered if Mother thought of Miss J as a sibling. But when Mother introduced me to Miss J later, she seemed to know that Miss J was not a sister or her mother. Later I asked Mother more about Miss J when we were in her room.
"Mother, how long have you known her?"
"Not long," Mother said, later indicating they had just met.

Mother still asked about home and going home, but there was an acceptance of where she was. A few words from the staff or me telling Mother that this place was her home seemed to satisfy her. I wondered if Miss J's friendship was part of Mother's better attitude. Perhaps

Mother just enjoyed the friendship with and attention from Miss J. I was grateful for Miss J being a friend to Mother. I still did not know if Mother and Miss J ever talked. But both seemed happier, though.

Am I Intruding?

I visited Mother on a Tuesday afternoon in mid-December and found her sitting in her place at the dinner table. Mrs. M was seated to Mother's left, and Miss J was hovering behind Mother. Several others were seated at their places.

"Hi, Mother," I said.

"I'm so glad you came to see me," she said.

I complimented her on her hair, which looked very nice. She told me that she had had a permanent a few days earlier.

"Do you want to go back to your room and visit a while?" I asked.

She didn't respond right away. Instead, she answered, "Well, we are going to eat dinner in a little bit."

"It is about an hour before you eat," I said.

"Well, some of the folks here have to eat early so they can get back home," Mother replied. (We did not get into that story.)

"There is a little time before you eat. Don't you want to visit in your room?"

"Can't we just do it here?" Mother finally asked, holding firm.

"Yes, I guess we can," I conceded.

It was clear that Mother was settled in, waiting for dinner, and we were not going to her room. I excused myself to go to her room to retrieve the eyeglass cleaning solution. I also wanted to pick up the bag of pictures and the AARP bulletin I had brought over but left in her room.

As I left the dining room, I heard Mrs. M ask Mother, "Is that your son?"

Mother was answering as I left hearing distance.

I returned, cleaned her glasses, and felt her hands.

"They feel pretty good—just a little cool," I said.

"Your hands are warm," Mother said.

She held onto my hand for a long time. I took out the picture of my brothers and me that I had shown Mother a week earlier. It was of the three of us taken for her 90th birthday.

"Do you remember this picture?" I asked.

"Yes," Mother said smiling.

Suddenly, Mrs. M spoke up. "Are those your boys?"

Mother seemed pleased to tell her that we were, as she handed with shaking hands the picture to Mrs. M. As Mrs. M looked at it closely, she said something to me along the lines of it being good to have pictures. I agreed.

Mother, Mrs. M, and I were having a conversation. I never knew how much the residents talked, as I did not see it very often. More pleasing, though, was the fact that Mother and Mrs. M were having a conversation. I wondered how much Mother interacted with her neighbors.

I took out another picture and asked, "Do you recognize anyone in this picture?"

"There is me," Mother said, pointing to her picture.

The photo of the family at the side of her old home place had been taken in about 1952. "Do you recognize anyone else?" I asked.

She did not. I pointed out that Dad was in the picture with the rest of family—all five of us. Mother seemed the most contented I had seen her since she arrived in Memory Care. Yes, there was some anxiety, but as I recovered from being rebuffed earlier in the day, I began to think about what had happened. Mother obviously was more contented, and maybe Miss J and Mrs. M, were like a family. Conversations did go on. Miss J and Mother were virtually inseparable now. Mother seemed to have found her place.

Christmas in Memory Care

My wife and I went over to Mother's place at 10:30 on Christmas morning. Someone fetched her from the Christmas carol-singing group in the activities room. As we waited in Mother's room for her to arrive, we looked at the new clothes my brothers had brought over earlier. She had gotten a red jacket and two sweaters—one pink, one black. My wife found the snowmen pin that we had given Mother earlier pinned to another jacket. We picked dead flowers off the poinsettia and resolved to take it home and try to save it. A few minutes later, I heard Mother ask if it was her brother who was there to see her.

I walked out into the hallway and greeted Mother. She looked good. She was dressed in a red sweater with a Christmas brooch. She smiled and thanked us for coming. This was a good day. We gave Mother her presents first: a box of Whitman's chocolates wrapped in red paper and a large bottle of Jergen's lotion. Mother struggled to open the wrappings on the chocolates, so we did it together—she knew it was something good to eat. When she tried to pull the bottle of lotion out of the Christmas gift bag, she commented on how big it was. It was too heavy for her to lift but she knew what it was.

Mother wanted a piece of the Whitman's. Acting like the parent, I tried to dissuade her, telling her that her dinner time was coming up soon, but she would not be put off. I relented, but I did tell her she could only have one piece. "No, we aren't going to do that," Mother insisted, indicating that she felt no limitations to her box of chocolates. The piece that Mother chose was a gummy one that stuck in her teeth and occupied her enough that she could not go back for more, at least not then.

I showed her pictures of her grandchildren and great-grandchildren from Christmas cards they had sent. I wanted to keep faces and names in front of her. I named each one. She seemed mildly interested. We sat silently for a while. Mother had a pleasant smile on her face. She thanked us for coming and seemed to be aware of Christmas. She mentioned that she was away from home this Christmas, something that "seldom happened." I heard sadness in her voice.

The thought occurred to me that Mother had been forgotten, but this wasn't true: a son and a grandson had visited Mother on Christmas Eve, and another son had visited a few days earlier and brought her a jacket. Many of her grandkids sent cards. What else could they do? Everyone would have been delighted to have Mother at their table for Christmas dinner, but those days were over. Everyone had said that a disruption in her routine would be a killer—for her, for staff, for me. But still, Mother was alone in her room with only us and only talk. We sat in silence again.

My wife suggested a walk. Mother walked a lot with Miss J, so I nixed that idea. My wife then suggested that I read the Christmas story in the Gospel of Luke. I thought that was a good idea and would be another Christmas happening and memory. Mother nixed that, saying softly but emphatically that she did not want me to read.

Mother began to doze off. I had advised my wife to bring a book as I anticipated Mother's napping. I had my *Newsweek* magazine. Mother napped, listing to her right side as she did when she slept, and drifted off into a deep sleep. Then suddenly, for no apparent reason, she woke up, looked at me, and smiled. Being the kind hostess she was, Mother would now have to have a conversation with her visitors.

"Well, I almost fell asleep," she said.

"Yes," I responded, "you almost fell asleep."

Then, she asked where Audie was. I told her I did not know, and then moved quickly to another subject. She dozed and awoke three or four times that morning.

Dinner time approached. A take-charge staff worker came to get Mother, who had been bumped to another table today since Mrs. M's daughter and son-in-law were joining her for lunch. Mother said she hated for us to go. She seemed clingy that day, but we said we needed to go. As the worker escorted Mother to the dining room, we said goodbye and left with the empty Christmas bags, the almost-dead poinsettia, and our books. Why didn't we stay and have lunch with Mother? Because it's not pleasant, I thought guiltily.

The Cousins Come to Visit

Three children of Mother's brother Gene called me to say they wanted to visit with Mother on a Sunday in January. Since there were so many of us, Mother's room could not hold us all. Instead, we all huddled as much as we could into a corner of the TV room. Mother said she recognized her nephews and niece, which I am inclined to believe. She sat with such a pleasant, even pleased look, on her face. She had a little difficulty in understanding some of the conversation, and I tried to repeat it for her.

I had some concerns. First, would too many visitors put her off and confuse her? Would too much family history confuse her? Fortunately, neither was a problem. Mother's niece and nephews had a wealth of knowledge about her family, the original house Granddad built in about 1911, the big house that Mother was raised in, and her home community. They told Mother about renovations to the old home place, the old barn, the building of the highway close by, and lots of other stuff. They told her about a time when they were concerned because they could not reach their mother during a tornado. This was because she was on her front porch talking to *my* Mother and watching the tornado pass by.

An earlier tornado had lifted one of the family mules and carried her away. The cousins relayed how Granddad later found Fannie grazing contently in a nearby pasture. The barn had to be rebuilt, though. Both of the stories brought much laughter. So, many stories and so much fun. Mother did not hear it all, but she was smiling pleasantly.

I was worried that Mother would tire easily, fall asleep, and miss a good visit. She usually fell asleep when *I* visited her. Mother dozed off after about 30 minutes, and we talked on among ourselves as she napped for several minutes. As she usually did during her afternoon naps, Mother quickly jerked open her eyes and said, "I almost fell asleep."

"Yes," I agreed, "you almost did."

The mules and Granddad's farming were a long-discussed topic. Fannie, of tornado fame, was mentioned, but none of us could think of the other mule's name. Mother could. Mother informed us that the mules were Fannie and Mollie.

My cousins stayed with Mother for about an hour and a half. She had two short naps and woke with a mischievous grin the second time saying that had said she heard everything we said. I do not believe for a minute she heard everything we said, but she wanted us to believe that she was totally involved and maybe still the head of the family.

As we began our goodbyes—this family never leaves on the first goodbye but has to work up to it—Mother thanked them all for coming and said to come back whenever they could. There was no doubt that Mother meant it, for she was the sweet aunt they had known all their lives. She was also a genuinely kind person to family members and others.

Confusion and Loss of Miss J

Mother seemed to be doing so well, and the cousins' visit was a high point. The Monday and Tuesday afterward, however, were downers. A brother visited Mother on Tuesday morning and commented that she remembered the cousins' visit and named, and missed, some of them.

On Wednesday, Mother seemed very confused. She was standing in front of the office door, just standing and waiting. If she did recognize me, she did not seem happy to see me. I sat with her awhile, and tried to comfort and convince her that she was okay. "You know, Mother, when we get older, we need some extra help," I said. "These folks here give you that help. They care for you and help you. You are doing great."

Mother agreed, as she most often did, and replied, "Yes, I guess you are right." She gradually calmed. She washed her hands (just barely), and we walked down to the dining room where her meal was waiting. She spoke to Miss J and Mrs. M, sat down, and kissed me goodbye.

Gina confirmed that Mother had been confused all week. I related about the cousins' visit and the possibility that the cousins may have pushed Mother back to a time when she was around family. The director added that Miss J had recently taken up with the dolls the center kept around, and that now dolls was Miss J's interest and Mother was not. It was impossible to know what triggered Mother's change; it might just be the nature of the disease.

Birthday Number 94

We celebrated Mother's 94th birthday on a Sunday in early February, almost two years into her stay in Memory Care. We invited all the residents to the party and served cake and ice cream. I had asked Mother what kind of cake she wanted. I allowed that I knew she did not like coconut cake, but she made it for others. Mother acknowledged that this was the case. She preferred a white cake with white icing. The bakery in a local grocery store made her such a cake, and piped "Happy Birthday, Mother, Grandmother, and Great-Grandmother" on the top. All representatives of those groups were present for Mother's birthday. Great-granddaughters marched the cake, with two lighted "9" and "4" candles, down the aisle to Mother while the group sang "Happy Birthday."

Knowing the propensity for Mother to enjoy cake (and many other sweets), someone had cut her a large piece. I supposed that such a piece would prevent the need to serve her three slices, as happened last year. Mother was served first. She began right away on the cake and continued unabated while others were served. It was a *huge* piece of cake. Mother was working hard and getting it eaten, but I feared she would have too much. I volunteered that she did not *have* to eat it all, if she did not want it. Mother looked at me and said nicely, but forcibly, "I am going to eat it all." And she did.

Quarterly Meeting on Mother and Learning the Language

Quarterly meetings are required by the state licensing board, so, Gina, the nurses and the staff who work with Mother, and my brothers and I all met in February. Mother had improved in some of the risk categories: Her risk of escaping the premises was low, and while she was diapered all the time now, she was not totally incontinent. Mother was participating in exercise; she had not fallen; she was ambulatory. She was doing well and was not in danger of getting booted from Memory Care. This was always a big concern and the basis for many of our questions.

A potential issue, and one with dire consequences, was brought up at the meeting, though: eating. One requirement of staying in Memory Care was for residents to feed themselves. The staff had been "illegally" cutting up Mother's food (they are not allowed to do that because of state rules against it), so the doctor had to order a "soft diet" for Mother. However, it was not the soft diet most people immediately think of; there were no grits, mashed potatoes, and soup. A doctor's order for a "soft diet" allowed food to be minced before serving, so then Mother could feed herself. It made sense when one knew the language. The nurse had already begun the soft diet project. She also wanted to have Mother examined by a speech therapist to assess Mother's swallowing and concerns about her throat. My brothers and I thought this idea was great; we had also learned a new role for a speech therapist.

At our meeting, Gina related the time Mother got angry with her and wanted the director to come to her room to explain why she (Mother) was there. Mother allowed that she did not know anything that was going on; she was again "lost." This feeling of not knowing where she was, of what to do, or where to go had reared its ugly head again. Gina tried to divert Mother to other activities, finally succeeding with a question on butterbeans. Gina said that she tried to go several directions before landing on the topic of butterbeans. Maybe it worked because Mother felt familiar with butterbeans. With butterbeans, she was not lost.

"I Could Sew"

As I entered the hallway to find Mother on a late March Sunday, a staff member said, "Here is the favorite son!" Mother looked good. Her hair was nicely groomed, and she had on light clothing. I told her so. She thanked me. I asked what she had done that day.

"I went to Sunday School and church," Mother told me.

I mentioned a brother's three paintings that he had hung in her room. I told Mother how nice they looked in there. She nodded approval and commented that she liked them too. Mother was not convincing that she really knew the paintings were there, but she might have. Launching from the paintings, I asked her if she had any artistic abilities. Could she paint or draw? Mother said she could not paint or draw, only sew. This word "sew" was the idea I was looking for.

"I could sew," Mother had said. And indeed, she could. She had worked at an earlier time for a shirt manufacturer and had made our pajamas and shirts until we boys got uppity and wanted store-bought things. We went way back in history this day, and I thought she remembered most of it correctly.

"Where did you get your first sewing machine?" I began.

"It was from Grandmother (Dad's mother)," Mother responded quickly. "She was not sewing much anymore."

"Did most everyone sew back then?"

"Yes, but some could do more than others."

"Did you learn to sew from your mother?"

"Yes."

"How did you do it?"

"There are patterns for dresses and shirts. I would get a pattern and material."

"What was the most difficult to sew?"

Mother stumbled here just a bit, and did not answer directly at first. I am not sure she knew what I meant. Eventually, she answered: "There were different patterns for dresses. There was only one pattern for pajamas." As we explored making dresses with different necklines and so forth, she allowed that dresses were harder to make: "I made coats, too. I sewed for others who could not do it."

As supper was announced and we closed out our conversation, I thought how good Mother had been in doing all those tasks: gardening, canning, cooking, and sewing. Everyone back then did them, but Mother seemed to excel. Today, she could remember this part of her life and what she did so well. Was it because a way-back memory was better remembered, or was it because sewing was ingrained and pleasing to her? I felt like we had opened a new door—one I had never really explored with Mother. It was almost like our conversations back before dementia. As we prepared to go to supper, I saw a gift bag and some candy wrappers.

"Did someone bring you some candy?" I asked

"I think Audie brought it," Mother replied.

Then, on the way to supper, I could see she did not want me to go: "I thought I would go home with you and eat tonight." I hurt again.

Whose Clothes Are These?

During a visit with Mother around Easter, she insisted that I share her candy, which I did. She wasted no time in getting to the candy, and we both wasted no time in finishing the package. We had messy hands from the milk chocolate-covered marshmallow Easter eggs. Mother mused, "We do not need to leave any of these around. They are too messy." Amen!

Mother was restless. She was not anxious, or sad, or very happy; she was just restless. I saw it in her face as she looked off and back. She got up one time to walk around her room, which she had never done before. She then walked back and forth once or twice and sat back down.

The theme of the day was her clothes and the fact that they did not fit. In fact, they may not have been *her* clothes at all. She wore a tan, leather-looking jacket over a lighter-tan blouse and black pants. "This jacket is too small. I don't think it's mine," Mother complained.

I looked in the neckline but did not see a name written in. I tried to convince Mother that it was her jacket and that someone had bought it for her.

"We need to find out," Mother replied, "so we can thank them."

I agreed. What else could I do?

"I don't think this jacket is mine," she said again a few minutes later. "I think it must be Danny's."

I told her, rather unconvincingly, that I thought it was hers.

Then she said she thought the blouse she was wearing was not hers, either. I checked the label and found her name there—twice. I told her that the blouse was hers and that her name was on it. I was more convincing on this garment.

Then we sat silently and stared a while.

Mother then asked, "Does Dan have an indoor toilet?"

I was not surprised now at any question, so I answered, "Yes, yes he does."

I could tell the reason she asked that question.

"It is right over there," I said pointing to her bathroom.

She apologized for needing to go to the bathroom at this time. As she walked into the bathroom, it was as though she was entering the room for the first time. Afterwards, she came out with her pants only partly up.

"These pants are too small," she said.

I looked at the label and saw 16P and knew they were a new pair that a brother and his wife had recently bought. I pulled them up over her Depends, and told her how nicely they fit.

Mother walked back to her chair and sat down. It was a few minutes before supper.

"What was Dan going to do today?" she asked.

"Oh, just catch up today and rest," I said.

"I am not sure these are my clothes I have on. I think this coat might be Dan's."

We left for supper.

What's the Use?

My wife saw this quote from novelist Kate Atkinson in her book *Behind the Scenes at the Museum*[3] and shared it with me: "Her lost self, incapable of enjoyment, would have balked at the amount of time we waste every day. I've waited forty years to play with my mother, and now at last we spend long sunny afternoons in an endless state of make-believe on planet Alzheimer."

I had been visiting Mother in Memory Care now for many months. I had seen good days of lucidity and bad days of utter confusion. And now, I was at an impasse. I questioned why I even visited Mother. I was pretty sure she did not remember my being with her, at least not outside of the time I was present. She was forgetting us, but I was searching for something. My question kept hounding me. What is the purpose in my visiting her?

About that time, Chaplain Mark of Memory Care directed me to John Swinton's book, *Dementia: Living in the Memories of God*[4]. Was it just coincidence that my awareness of this book came while I was questioning myself? Swinton writes the counter-story to Alzheimer's disease. He does not doubt any of the medical evidence, the debilitation, or sadness arising from the disease, but he also calls attention to the inner *self*, the *self* we no longer recognize, the *self* negatively positioned by society. Then, he pushes his idea to the caregivers and to their job.

Swinton offers further probing questions: What if you know who you are but are just confused and cannot remember? Who will I be when I have forgotten who I think I am? He writes, "The loss of memory in dementia entails a loss of *self*, and we can no longer be secure in our notions of 'self-fulfillment.'" This comment struck a chord with me. Mother, born in the era of the "Greatest Generation," had lost her confidence. In fact, she *was* lost.

"Do you think I am cold? Do I need a sweater?" were not unusual questions of late. Dementia, possibly Alzheimer's, had taken away the Mother I recognized. Her loss of confidence was only one sign. She was not sure what she knew. Swinton calls on caregivers to "find the means and insight to see [the *self*] and to recognize its presence and to stay with it effectively."

I had seen Mother's *self,* usually in our talks about gardening, canning, sewing, or things she knew and loved. She was more like her old *self* at these times. Some folks call it "moments of lucidity," although such moments are often a confusion of facts, names, and events. Mother related to home and family stories; with them, her own story was clearer. But I *also* saw Mother in her demeanor, in her kindness to me and others, and in her rambling statements that often contained the truth of life's experiences.

But what about, as Swinton despairingly labels it, negative positioning by society? In Swinton's example, a wife introduces her husband John with the statement, "He has dementia." John had lost his former position in society, his identity. This story weighed on my mind. Not long after reading the story of John, I came upon some interesting old photos when visiting a flea market in a state park. As I looked through several of them, an old man came up to me and began talking about the people in the pictures. Nearby, a woman chimed in, "He's got Alzheimer's." She probably meant, "Don't pay any attention to him. He should not be taken into account." I felt sad for him, and I remembered Swinton's caution of society's negative positioning of such people. I had no idea if he really knew the folks in the picture or not, but he never got a chance to tell me.

At the close of Swinton's book, which is unabashedly religious, he wrote, "The sadness of dementia need not and indeed must not be allowed to have the final word. Even in the midst of the pain and affliction that can accompany dementia, there are hidden possibilities if we trust God and allow the challenge of our sadness to stimulate new ways of thinking and being with one another."

Swinton's words had an impact. I tried to listen to Mother, to her story, more openly, but what should I do with stories that are confused and likely not factual? I felt guilt and sadness so often when I visited Mother that sometimes I just did not want to go. I expected the visits would get harder.

Why *did* I visit Mother? Perhaps I was trying to reflect Swinton's premise that Mother's *self* still remained intact and could be encountered if I could "find the means and insight to see it and to recognize its presence and to stay with it effectively." I could see her in some moments, even in her anger when things were not right. Or maybe I visited Mother because I knew she would have wanted me to, and it brought her some pleasure. As Mother would say, "You do what you ought to do." Or maybe it was another call, one heard by those claiming faith.

For as Jesus tells us in parables, "And the king will answer them, 'Truly I tell you, just as you did it to one of the least of these who are members of my family, you did it to me'" (Matt. 25-40). Alzheimer's sufferers, to quote Swinton, are "negatively positioned by society" and seem to be among "the least of these."

I Need to See Mother Anew

In addition to Swinton's book, Chaplain Mark introduced me to Frederick A. Trunk's *Alzheimer's/Dementia: From the Experiences of a Caregiver*.[5] Both books were Christian in nature and contained practical guidance—particularly Trunk's little 62-page journey with his wife. Both books helped me answer the question, "Why am I visiting Mother?" Swinton and Trunk stressed the importance of visiting people with dementia. Swinton in particular stressed the humanness of dementia sufferers and that they should be treated with respect and dignity. They should be listened to, but in a different way than before. With ideas from these books in mind, I began to see Mother differently; I think I began to see myself differently in our relationship too. So, while Mother might not say or do things the same as before, the onus was on me to adapt.

I had been away for about 10 days before I saw Mother at our normal time on Sunday, the last day of June. She was sitting at her place in the dining room. She recognized me and was very aware that her neighbor was also seated there. "Do you know …" Mother began but could not finish the introduction.

It was clear that she was trying to acknowledge me to her neighbor, even though the names and sentences would not come through. Is this what Swinton was getting at? In some way, Mother was who she always had been. She was trying to be a kind, thoughtful person wanting to acknowledge everyone.

"Yes," I helped out. "I know her. How are you today?"

The neighbor did not respond.

And then there was the new staff member who was just getting Mother up from the dining table when I came to visit. As most staff there did, the new worker had praise for how sweet and kind Mother was. Then, the worker surprised me: "She is always talking about her boys. She tells me your names and about growing up. She says you were good boys and tried to be good. She mentioned the jewelry store and her husband's name. That's it, E.G."

I was surprised—amazed, really. Just when I thought Mother might be forgetting everything, I heard how much she remembered, what was important to her, and how much she wanted to share with others. Mother was always who she had been, just different now.

What a Difference Three Days Make

On an August Sunday I stopped by Mother's room before I went looking for her. Her bed was unmade, which was very unusual. Her watch and necklace were on the bathroom counter, which was also unusual. I put a recently picked zinnia on the dresser and went to look for her.

Mother was walking to her chair in the dining room. She looked awful! Her hair was not combed, her clothes were not up to par, and she looked lost and bewildered. She had a device tethered from her blouse to her walker. A staff member quickly explained that the device would produce a loud beep when the connection was broken—that is, when Mother left her walker. "She keeps walking away from it," the worker explained.

I had found out on Friday that Mother had a urinary tract infection again and was on antibiotics. Perhaps the medicine had not kicked in yet, and Mother was still suffering from the infection. Also, the weekend nurse said that Mother had slept until noon and gotten up only at their insistence. It was not one of Mother's better days.

Three days later on Wednesday, Mother was 180 degrees different from Sunday. She was just getting up from her chair in the dining room when I arrived. The staff was gathered around; the nurse was laughing and said that Mother had set off the beeper. She said Mother did not want that thing on her and had just pulled it off. (Good for Mother!)

I left the device unclipped and walked with her back to her room. Mother looked so good today. She was smiling and happy and cheerful. As she sat in her chair, I noticed that she had bangs. Her hair had been shampooed and set by the beautician there earlier in the week. The bangs made her look about 20 years younger. Her nails had been manicured and a clear polish applied rather than the hot red. Mother had on a deep blue sweater with a matching purple and blue jacket and blue pants. But it was her expression that was so different today. She looked happy and felt good. She had responded to the medicine for the urinary tract infection.

We talked about gardening and harvesting, and the pleasure when the garden begins to play out and less harvesting is required. She smiled as if she knew that well. I told Mother she had not felt well on Sunday and was taking some medicine. Now she seemed better. She never said she felt bad on Sunday—either she was stoic or she did not know she felt bad, I am not sure which. Mother almost never complained because she said that folks didn't like it.

After a deep sleep (she didn't even hear the high-powered blower used by the yard men outside her window), she woke with a smile on her face. "Supper already?" she said with anticipation. I combed her hair a bit, just to fuss over her some, remarking that her hair looked good. I didn't need to comb much, but she was pleased with the attention. As we walked to dinner, she did not say "I am not hungry." What a difference three days (and medicine) made.

Last Food of the Day

"I am afraid," Mother said carefully on a Wednesday visit in September.

"Afraid?" I repeated. "Mother, what are you afraid of?"

"I don't know anything," she allowed.

As usual, I tried to reassure her that everything was okay—paltry words for a feeling when you do not know where you are, why you are there, and who the people are around you. She *was* afraid. The only thing I knew to do was sit with her a while and try to guide her in another direction that was less unsettling. This act seemed paltry too.

Mother, though, seemed to respond a bit. She at least had her son, whom she remembered. In fact, she asked about her other sons. She remembered us all. She did not say she wanted to go home; she just wanted to know something about herself. That memory was lost. Despite this feeling, the kindness of Mother showed through in glimpses.

"I don't want you to be hindered by me," she said, indicating she was aware of her state and my doing for her. Of course, I told her she was not a "hinder" to me. That statement was mostly true: Coming to visit her and doing the small amount of financial work was no hinder; the hinder was seeing her as she was and not being able to help. For the first time, she refused to eat dinner.

"I just ate. I am not hungry," Mother insisted more than once.

As the staff served her brightly colored food in a curved bowl, I wondered how much she could see of the orange carrots, white potatoes, and brown meat. Mother sat and looked at the food; she insisted she was not hungry. I told her it was fine to not eat—it was okay. I told her to just eat what she liked, or nothing. Mother was not at peace with this idea. She knew she was *supposed* to eat.

"I don't want to create a problem," she finally said.

Mother continued to be concerned for the others, in this case, the staff who had prepared the food. Growing up as she did and being a homemaker for years, Mother knew you did not waste food. I believe these ideas were behind her concern.

Then Mother asked, "Will I have some food later?"

"No," I said. "I think this will be all the food until breakfast tomorrow."

Mother pursed her lips, as if she were considering this proposal, then she took a few bites of carrots. I thought that she showed some signs of lucidity and logic. She was still kind and not wanting to be a hinder or a nuisance. She also realized this was the last food for today.

Quarterly Meeting

In early September the nurse's report on Mother confirmed our overall observations but provided details from the staff's position. Mother was getting weaker physically, although her blood pressure and weight were holding their own. However, she could no longer bathe herself; she was incontinent for urinary functions but not bowel functions; and she had to be brought to supper.

Mother's swallowing had become more problematic in the last three months. She choked on her pills, so now with a doctor's prescription the staff ground her pills and put them in pudding or apple sauce. The brothers and I thought that was not bad. Mother loved dessert anyway. Could this have been Mother's plan all along? The fact was that Mother required more personal care.

While all this information confirmed our view sand concerns, the good news was that Mother was doing everything required to stay in her residence.

Mother's Afternoons

Mother was talking to Kevin the nurse at the office door. Kevin was pleased to see me and passed Mother right over to me. We talked in her room for a while. "Is Danny here later today?" Mother asked.

Perhaps the staff had told her that I would be there but had not yet arrived. I told Mother of my days and events and that I had traveled away the day before. At some point, Mother told me that "Danny had to go to … a house yesterday." I noticed that Mother would pick up on a word or phrase and return to some form of it later on. That was the case, I think, with her comment about Danny. She had done this returning to topics a lot, I noticed. While she seemed to "remember" an event for a short time, she could not get the facts straight, and the topic was much confused. But it seemed she did "remember" something.

At the dementia support group meeting on Thursday, Chaplain Mark and others discussed situations related to loved ones with dementia. Many in the group were dealing with family members in the early stages of the disease (mostly older parents at home), and a common finding was that the dementia caused sufferers to repeat the same question repeatedly in short order. Mother also tended to repeat things when she first got sick and had low sodium levels. But her repeats were different from now, when she repeated a single word or phrase. Before, Mother kept asking why *this* happened and did anyone notice. Back then, Mother's repeating was a search for answers.

On a Sunday afternoon in early November, I found Mother sitting alone in the dining room. She smiled when she saw me and asked where I had come from. She seemed happy to see me and looked very smart in a white cardigan sweater with a leaf brooch. In front of her was a coffee cup, turned upside down on its saucer. As we talked, Mother kept reaching for and at times touching the cup. She did not know what it was. I told her it was a coffee cup and asked if she had had coffee.

"No," Mother replied. "I didn't."

"Do you want some coffee?" I then asked.

"No," she said.

"Is that a sugar bowl?" Mother asked just a little later.

I repeated that it was a coffee cup. She acknowledged that she understood, but a few minutes later she asked again about the coffee cup and what it was. Her repeating today resembled somewhat the reports I had heard in the support group session. It was no longer research; it was just repeating.

I was silent, but Mother seemed to enjoy sitting there with company. The staff brought her dinner soon after supper began: minced meat, white potatoes, and sweet potatoes. The three portions were neatly placed in the curved, white plate that was Mother's dish. I think we both felt the tension when supper arrived.

"Mother, I have to go," I said.

"I don't what you to go," she responded.

"I need to go and run some errands," I lied.

"I don't want you to go and leave me alone," she confided.

I think she hit directly on the issue—she did not want to be alone. When her table was full of folks, I could leave rather easily. When no one else was present, and the room was only partially full, Mother felt lonely. And she did not want to be alone.

"I know, Mother, but I need to go," I repeated.

Mother pursed her lips together, stared straight ahead, and said nothing. Her face was a face of … disappointment, or sadness, of betrayal, or maybe all of those things. She held that position for a while, saying nothing and not changing her expression. I felt sorry for her, and I could do nothing to help other than stay.

"Mother," I said, "I love you, but I have to go."

I hovered over her a bit, just looking at her and holding her hand. Finally, she gave in and told me she loved me too. But I could see her disappointment that she would be alone now. As I was leaving, a staff member asked if I wanted him to move Mother to a table with others. I said that would be nice. As I left, I glanced back at Mother. Another worker was sitting with her and talking to her. Thank you, I thought. But I felt terrible.

"I Wish I Could Go Home With You"

Mark Twain wrote, "There is nothing to be learned from the second kick of a mule." This saying caught my attention since it seemed like we had been in this situation before but had not learned much. Mother, once again, wanted to go home, but there was no home to go to, and even if there was, she could not live there. I was being kicked by a mule for the second time.

For the last few visits, Mother had talked of going home or going home with one of us. Her tablemates had all left, or not come to dinner, so she sat alone. When Mother went to the dining room in the afternoon, she sat alone. When she went to her room, she was alone. Mother was alone most all the time, and she was lonely. That was my take on this latest need to go home. So, if that was the problem, what was the solution?

There was a table full of women who always sat together. Sometimes, when Mother was alone or when I brought her down and no one was present at her table, the staff would seat Mother with John. I don't think Mother and John talked or shared any particular bond. Perhaps, however, this situation was better than being alone.

The visit on Sunday in mid-November was a downer. Mother was in her chair in her room and awake. "Is that Dan?" she asked when she saw me. I was not sure if the question was real or rhetorical. Did she recognize me? She was pleased to see me, though. We talked a little, but it was hard for Mother to hear today. She indicated a couple of times that someone—I did not know who—had come and taken a nap in her room today. She mentioned it twice, then said she *thought* it happened. (It could have, as one of my brothers discovered a man in her bed one day—it had been his old room.) She sat silently most of the time.

But there were moments. Mother was fiddling with getting a small bit of food from her mouth. She kept on rubbing her sweater over her mouth, and I got her a tissue.

"Is there something in your mouth?" I asked.

"Yes, something other than my tongue," Mother replied as she smiled at me.

I liked her joke, and it made me see that she was more aware at times than I realized. I told her that I had talked to my children that day, reminded Mother of who they were, and added, "They are adults now, and I do not tell them what to do. They would not listen anyway."

"They listen more than you realize," Mother replied wisely.

As we finished getting ready to go to dinner and started out of the door, Mother said, "I wish I could go home with you." It felt like both kicks of the mule.

"No, I'm Not Cold, But This Sweater Sure Feels Good"

Mother was sitting in the dining room on Sunday in mid-November, although in her neighbor's seat. She smiled sweetly when she saw me. She was wearing a short-sleeved blouse with her arms exposed.

"Aren't you cold?" I asked. "Let me get your sweater."

"No, I am alright," Mother replied, not really convincing me that she was not cold.

I repeated my offer, and she refused again. It was as though she did not want me to leave. Finally, I told her that I would just go down the hall to her room to fetch the sweater and would be right back. I did not wait for approval. I helped her put the pink sweater on, pulling it down in back when she stood up. She was pleased to have her sweater, and she said she was warm.

Around 4:30 p.m., folks began gathering for dinner. A worker was distributing placemats and silverware to the tables. Mother's next move was the saddest I had observed in a long time: She picked up her fork and then tried to pick up her "food," lifting my handkerchief with the fork. Finally, I had to tell her that the food had not come out yet. Mother tried two more times within a few minutes to pick up her food, once with her fork and once with her spoon. I reminded her again that the food had not arrived. She put her spoon down and said, "Oh."

There was no embarrassment on her part; there was nothing. She just put her spoon down. Then all of a sudden, her tablemate was there and joined us. It was just as if she had "appeared"—or maybe I just thought she was angelic! While Mother did not say anything or change her blank expression, I believe she was pleased that her tablemate was there. I, on the other hand, was *delighted* to see this woman and Mother's happy attitude today. I knew Mother would feel some comfort having her tablemate around, but she still did not want me to leave.

Mother Finishes Off the Year on a Good Note

Mother had been in Memory Care for just under three years. She was bright, alert, and interactive most of those times, and I continued my regular schedule of visits through Christmas and New Year.

On Christmas Day, my wife and I visited Mother and brought her gifts. I gave her the first one, a rectangular box neatly wrapped by Mr. Russell Stover.

"What do you think it is?" I playfully asked her.

"It looks like a box of candy." Mother responded.

I helped her open the box, and her face showed pleasure. "Let's have a piece," she said.

Mother wanted to make sure that "Winnie" got a piece of candy. Calling my wife "Winnie" was one of the few missteps that day, but even then Mother seemed unsure if "Winnie" was correct.

I repeated my question to her for her second gift. "It looks like a blouse," Mother said, again guessing the general nature of the gift.

We opened the package, and I showed Mother a new gray sweater. I could tell she liked that gift as well. "That will be so warm," she said with a smile. Mother was into Christmas, but she felt bad that she had not gotten us a gift. Her kindness and concern for others was still a part of her. John Swinton would say it was that part of the *self* still present.

On the last Sunday in December, Mother and I took a walk around the hallway. It was another good day. Was Mother improving? She was certainly holding her own, and her evaluation agreed.

Earlier in the month I had received the new format for quarterly reports on Mother. Her reports would now be a document instead of a visit by her three sons with the staff. Mother's blood pressure and weight had remained steady, and according to the attached narrative, Mother was at no higher risk of eloping than she had been in the previous quarter. Her fall risk was less; she had no "behavioral concerns," and scored 40 percent in "socialization/activation participation." The last comment was nicely put by the nurse: "Resident alert/pleasantly confused. Enjoys sleeping in. Tolerates diet well. Frequent safety checks and roller walker reminders given."

Birthday Number 95

We had been talking this day up for some time. How much Mother remembered from announcement to announcement of her birthday I did not know, but she said "Yes, I've been told that." We celebrated her birthday three days early on Sunday, January 26.

In trying to build up this event, I had pressed Mother on several occasions as to what kind of cake she wanted. She would turn the question and ask me what I wanted. I never got a response. For her 94th birthday she wanted a white cake with butter frosting. But now she would not, or could not, tell me what she wanted. I ordered a cake from the bakery, but this time I went for chocolate cake with white icing. I left off all the "Mother, Grandmother, Great-Grandmother" salutations from last year and went with a plain "Happy Birthday." We had two candles making out the "95."

When I got to the dining room, the tables were set long ways, and several residents were already seated—and waiting. I was pleased that we could provide a party. The staff said more than once how much the folks there looked forward to such events. Mother was feeling pretty good. She had come to accept being the center of attention instead of shying away from such things, or at least I thought she did. Several of the residents came up to Mother and told her "Happy Birthday." Family members gave her gifts of a pink sweater, lotion, socks, and flowers.

At some point, Mother's family began leaving. She had always hated when folks had to leave and still did. My wife and I stayed around for another hour or so. We reviewed Mother's afternoon and the gifts she had received. She was very appreciative and excited all over again. We told her who of the family had come. While Mother was a bit subdued, she was very pleased. My son asked me later if his grandmother knew who he was. I told him I doubted she could recall his name but she knew he belonged and was delighted he came to her party.

As Mother, my wife, and I sat that warm Sunday afternoon in her room and regaled about the party, Mother wandered off a time or two, once asking about $10 and if it was enough. We had not mentioned money.

"I think it was enough," I said, without a clue as to what we were discussing.

"Well, I just wanted to make sure that we paid …," she continued until I interrupted her.

"Oh," I said, "that has already been taken care of and paid for."

The fact that whatever she was thinking about had already been done satisfied her. Mother had not lost her concern for paying her debts and seeing that everything was tidy. This was another Swinton moment of *self*.

We took Mother down to the dining room. The tables were still arranged as they had been for the party, not as they usually were for dinner. Mother sat across from her next-door neighbor Effie and Mrs. Mills. Both of the ladies talked a bit, and I thought Mother might be okay for us to leave.

"We have to leave now."

"I don't want you to go," Mother said with a pouty look. She had always hated goodbyes and the family leaving. And she still hated it.

"Happy 95th birthday, Mother."

"I Sang Happy Birthday to Myself"

On the day before Mother's actual 95th birthday, we had the worst snowstorm in a long time. Wednesday morning was cold, 21 degrees, with lots of snow and ice all around. By 4 p.m., though, the roads were clear, and off I went to visit Mother on her actual birthday.

She was seated at her place in the dining room. She already had her purple bib on. I asked Mother if she knew it had snowed. She indicated she did not know but knew it was cold. I had been remiss and forgotten to pull a piece of her chocolate birthday cake from the freezer and had no time to pick anything up at the store. Instead, I borrowed some cookies from my wife's charity group. Mother enjoyed the light, fluffy one, reaching and putting fragments in her mouth non-stop until it was all eaten.

A worker came over and rounded up a singing group among the residents. We all sang "Happy Birthday" to Mother. She enjoyed the recognition. After all the singing, she looked at me and said with a smile, "I sang 'Happy Birthday' to myself. I guess that is okay."

I said it was indeed.

Mother was the last one served for dinner, but with an apology thinking that she had already been served. Mother did not say anything but seemed pleasant. I had to go, but Mother told me that the food would not be as good if I left. With the horrible weather outside, the staff rushing to get hot food to everyone, and Mother's sunny room waiting for her with her own warm bed and quilts for later, I felt thankful that Mother was there and not back in her old home by herself.

At Last: A Celebrity!

"Dan, this is Courtney," the voice on the other end of the line said. At first, I could not think who Courtney was, but about the time my mind engaged and I remembered that she worked at the retirement center, Courtney blurted out, "Your mother is alright! Your mother is alright!"

Although she was still young, Courtney was experienced enough to know that a call from her to a resident's family could be feared as the "last call," so she quickly let me know this was not *that* call. "We would like to take a picture of your mother and the director, for promotional purposes," Courtney continued. "Every morning the director kisses your mother on her forehead, and they say how much they love each other. Would it be alright if we took a picture?"

I could envision that scene. In a later conversation, the director told me that they tried to "out love" each other, with one saying "I love you" and the other responding "I love you more." I was pleased that the center saw the joy in this interaction and wanted to capture it, even if it was to make a little money for the organization.

"Of course, you can. That would great," I said. When I went to sign for the approval for the picture, I was told that the picture of Mother and the director would be one of two the center would submit to their national office. Mother was a celebrity! And it only took 95 years!

Birthday Cake and Cake and Cake …

Mother had a lot of birthday cake left over from her 95th party. This overage was despite our inviting all the residents and a boatload of family. Still, there was a third of the cake left. As a result of Mother's advice and habits during my upbringing, I wrapped the cake as well as I could and froze it.

In February, I unwrapped the cake, cut off a piece, and took it to Mother on a Sunday visit. She jumped right in. Although she hated to eat cake if I was not also going to have a piece, she did not hate it for long. Mother briefly asked if I wanted some. But while she was asking, she kept sampling the icing with her finger. I told her to enjoy the cake and that I did not want any.

I thought this was a good idea, so, I cut her a piece for the next visit, except I cut a slice considerably larger than the first one.

Mother and Betsy were seated across from each other at their dining table. I do not think there was any conversation. Mother was happy to see me. Betsy and I exchanged greetings. Then, I showed Mother the piece of cake. I do not recall any hesitancy to start right in on it.

Betsy, very practically minded, said, "She won't want any supper."

Oh yes, she will, I thought. And even if she doesn't, who cares. Everyone would rather eat cake than broccoli. What better time for such than when you are 95? Betsy declined the offer of some cake, perhaps thinking of *her* supper. Mother's arm was almost automatic in its movement to the cake, to the mouth, to the cake. If a morsel of cake did not make it onto the spoon, Mother still lifted the spoon to her mouth and then back again. Her movements were slow, measured, and persistent. This action went on until the entire piece was eaten—no stops. I think Betsy and I were both amazed that Mother finished off the cake without stopping to rest.

"How was it?" I asked after she had finished.

"It was good," Mother replied. "Just not enough."

Of course not, I thought. There could never be enough cake.

Supper was a bit later that evening, which was fortuitous since Mother was not hungry. But when the staff brought her curled plate, Mother immediately began the perpetual motion of spoon in food, spoon to mouth, spoon in food. It seemed that the cake had not ruined her supper after all. This episode taught me a lesson I cannot share with my granddaughters quite yet: that it is never too close to supper for cake.

Last One Standing

The obituary announced that the last remaining spouse of Dad's eight brothers had died. My aunt had not been well for several years, living in a nursing home under the watch of her daughter. Her death was not unexpected; in fact, it was a relief for all, including her I assumed. Adhering to the practice we established a few years back, I did not tell Mother of her sister-in-law's passing.

It dawned on me that Mother was now the last remaining member of Dad's family. For a few years she had been the sole survivor of her own family of siblings and spouses. Mother was now the sole survivor of two important families of her growing-up community. She was the last one standing.

February and March Musings

March was Mother's three-year anniversary in Memory Care. I was able to keep the Sunday and Wednesday visiting schedule for some time. On this visit, I talked with Mother about some consulting work I was doing and that I would be doing more of it. Mother, though, took the idea of work and turned it into the topic of sports. Since all three of her sons had engaged in all sorts of ball—football, baseball, and basketball—she equated what I was doing, no matter what it really was, with playing ball.

"Dan plays some ball but wants to play more," Mother said, reflecting on my comment of work and wanting to do more. Let's go with the subject of ball, I thought, so I asked Mother about playing ball herself. "Tam ball," she said.

I remembered Mother teaching me about tam ball. The way we played it was to hit, not tag, the runner with the ball when he or she was off base for an out. When I tried to pursue this line, Mother did not have much to say, so I told her that I made the soft balls we used out of string. I usually had several to play with. "If it has several balls in it, it can get expensive," she said.

On a later visit, I woke Mother from her nap in the sitting room. She smiled warmly. We talked of my returning from a trip to Canada. "I know your mother is glad you are home," she told me, then added, "You have a big family and I have a big family. It is good to be with everyone."

"I don't know where to stay," she continued. "I don't want to take someone else's bed."

Some days Mother was more lucid, such as during my visit in early March. I commented on having to trim back the crape myrtles we had at home. I said I did not think we had such plants when I was growing up. Mother kindly corrected me that we did and we had lots of them.

"They are easy to grow," she added. And she was certainly right about that.

I said something about forgetting.

"You do not forget as much as I do," she lamented.

Mother seemed very stooped on this visit. Her neck was bent forward; her hair was fine and soft; her hands were old with prominent veins. I told her that today was Transfiguration Sunday in the church. She looked perplexed. I repeated what I said, thinking she did not hear me. Then, sadly, this very religious woman said, "I don't think I know that story." I was truly sorry that she was forgetting even her long-remembered stories of Jesus.

"I Was Thinking How Nice It Was That You Visited Me Today"

Mother was in the activities room on a Thursday in late March, alone and sound asleep. I gently touched her hand to wake her. She woke with a smile and said, "I have the key in my hand." I did not know the story in her mind at that time, but her thoughts seemed vivid to her.

We took a stroll down the hallway on the way to her room. She was so pleasant today, and I had the feeling she felt this was home. She thanked me for visiting her.

A brother related how he and Mother had talked about a hog killing and about Easter egg hunts in earlier times. I asked Mother about their conversation to determine if the "hog-killing story" would stay with her for more than a day; it did not. My question drew a blank expression. Neither did she recall the Easter egg hunt story. In fact, she asked if she had seen my brother when he came by. This was typical for my brother's visits to Mother and, I strongly suspected, for mine as well.

Mother was enjoying the view out of her window. She had a smile on her face, and I wondered what she was thinking, so I asked her. "I was thinking how nice it was that you visited me today, and I hope (here she stumbled on words) … that we can visit again," she said. I thought that she was all in the moment now, and with family. It was a special day with her.

Sunday and More Cake and More Church

On the last Sunday in March, Mother was in her chair asleep, or at least very drowsy. When I spoke to her, she opened her eyes and asked who it was. She was pleased to see me and said how handy this little room was. I guess she meant for our meeting.

I watered her plants, cleaned her glasses, held her hands a bit, and talked. Then, I told her I had a surprise—a piece of her birthday cake that I had saved in the freezer. As I had done for the last three visits, I fed Mother the cake. She finished the entire piece, slowly and enjoying each bite.

She did not look well. After sleeping "all day yesterday," according to the weekend nurse, Mother had gotten up early. It was noticeable that she was sleeping more and had slept during most of my stay on Wednesday. She was very slow and mostly looked through the window, seemingly far off. I asked her if she felt okay. She said she did, but I think her answer was just the response she usually gave and was not how she really felt. She had told Chaplain Mark earlier that day that she did not feel well and she needed to go home.

As we sat together and talked some, Mother said that Audie had told her that she did not look like she felt well today and that she should rest after church. "That is what I did," Mother said.

We sat silently most of the visit. Soon, it was time to begin to move toward the Sunday afternoon church service that Chaplain Mark held, but Mother did not want to go. As I stood over her, waiting, she slowly began to move. Then she grabbed her pants, a signal that she needed to use the bathroom. Today was more of an effort to get this act accomplished, but she did, and we walked to the church service.

We were late. All the chairs at the table were taken, so was overflow space behind the chaplain. I moved a chair out to a spot where Mother could see.

"I need to go now," I said.

"Who will get me back?" Mother asked.

"The workers here will get you to supper and where you need to go, just like always," I told her.

Mother looked at me with pitiful eyes and said, "I don't want you to go. Stay with me."

Her statement hurt. While she often said this to me when I left, today it seemed like she really felt alone. Mother was with 25 or more of her residence mates, and the chaplain was already praying about the Lenten season. It was always a struggle to leave at times like this, and when I did, I did not feel good myself.

I Had Been Expecting This

Mother was sitting in the activities room with several other ladies doing puzzles on a Sunday in early April. Actually, two of the ladies were doing puzzles; Mother was picking up puzzle pieces and putting them in a box. Her focus on picking up the puzzle pieces reminded me of her focus on separating the various colored straws some time back. It was an assigned job that she was going to do and finish. And she did, picking up every piece and then looking around to be sure she had them all.

"What are you doing?" I asked as I sat next to her.

"Well, I think this is what we are supposed to do," Mother said haltingly.

Her response was unusual. She did not say my name or anything about my coming to see her like she usually would. A few moments of sitting quietly next to Mother as she continued to pick up puzzle pieces caused me to think that she did not know me.

"Would you like for the lady to trim your nails?" I asked.

"No, I don't want them trimmed. They will be too long," Mother replied.

"Trimming will make them shorter," I continued.

"No, I don't want my nails cut," Mother said emphatically.

I did not continue with the discussion for fear of agitating her. I knew something was not right. I sat by her as she looked ahead and not at me.

"Did you sleep late today?" I finally asked.

"Not too late," Mother responded.

I found out later from the nurse that she had slept until the afternoon and had not been up long before I arrived. After Mother's short response, she was silent again. Mother gave no indication that I was present. It was like I was a stranger to her. When I spoke, she responded politely, as she did to everyone. Finally, I tried a different tack.

"Have you heard from your sons?" I asked.

"I hear from them every week," Mother replied quickly.

"Have you heard from Dan today?" I asked.

"No, I have not heard from Dan."

"Mother, I am Dan," I said.

Mother had a strange look on her face as she responded, "I don't recognize you."

I thought, hoped really, that Mother had not seen me well, so I moved to give her a good frontal view of me.

"I don't recognize you," Mother repeated.

"I am your Dan," I said.

"I am your Dan?" Mother asked by repeating my words as if she could say the words but not decode their meaning.

"Yes, I am your Dan," I said to her again.

"No, you are not my Dan," Mother replied.

"I am Dan," I repeated.

"You are not my Dan," Mother said more emphatically.

I stopped at that point.

Sad as this visit was, at least it was easier this time to leave.

Wednesday Visitation

Three days later, Mother recognized me again, smiled, and called my name. I was pleased that she knew who I was. She preferred to stay in the TV room rather than going to her room. The staff said that earlier she had been sitting at her table after lunch all alone. When the staff asked if she wanted to move, she replied that she was okay, just sitting there and "watching the children." She seemed to be in her own mind today.

For the better part of my visit, I just held her hand. She would squeeze my hand gently at times and touch her lips occasionally, but most of the time she just sat silently.

When dinner was announced, I asked a worker to take Mother to the table so I could leave. I thought there might be less of a "situation" when I left. But Mother still said she wished I would not leave. I told her I had to leave because I was on my way to church, thinking that I might get a break from the guilt—and I did. Mother seemed to be okay with my reason for leaving. I did go to church.

Later that evening, the preacher sent an email announcing the death of ML. The only information provided was that she had died at the retirement center. I thought how quickly ML seemed to fade. Did Mother know?

Two Good Results

On Wednesday, the last day of April, Mother was slumped over to her right, sound asleep. I called her name several times before she awoke.

"I didn't know you were sleeping so hard … if I had known you were here," Mother said. She transposed us, having the sleeper and the visitor confused, but in fairness I had just awakened her from a heavy slumber. Since my red, fold-up chair was not in its place, I asked Mother if a brother had been over visiting.

"Yes, he was here last night and yesterday," she said. "I haven't seen him today. He went with us to see our boys." Mother was in a different world today.

I told Mother I had fixed the ball-bearing rocker arm on our porch glider. My explanation got a lot longer and more complicated that I had intended, and I lost Mother somewhere along the way. But being the supportive mother that she had always been, she said, "It is good you did it for yourself."

Of course, we talked about the weather. I told her of the high winds and blown-over trees. Not to be outdone, Mother told me that she had had a hard rain around noontime. It had not rained for two days, but I did not contradict her, and in fact I *acknowledged* the rain.

"When everything will be better and I can go home, they will like it," Mother said.

"Who will like it," I asked, not knowing where we were just now.

"The girls," Mother continued.

I think she meant the staff. It was as though she was visiting them for a while, and they were ready for her to leave. She was dozing a lot of the time and slept hard at one point. Then she roused and smiled at me.

"Were you dreaming?" I asked.

"I don't know."

"I thought you might have been, since you were smiling."

"Maybe I was," Mother agreed.

She then asked, "Did you have a good time while you were away?" It had been three days since I saw her, so her question was valid.

"It was okay, but I didn't do too much," I said playing along.

Then she said the sweetest, most motherly thing in this made-up story: "I thought about you, but I didn't know anything I should do." Even in her fantasy world, Mother still showed her *self*. She went back to sleep.

I watched her for a while, the rise and fall of her chest and the regular respiration of her lungs. I wondered if one day she would simply stop breathing. The kind social director made reference to a time when Mother would pass from the retirement center to heaven. That was our hope, too.

Mother's new doctor knocked on her door. He was personable and knowledgeable about Mother and her history, including her stay at the psychiatric clinic. He examined Mother and said everything was fine. Her blood work was good too. He knew Mother was eating well but sleeping a lot. He wanted to reduce the calming medicine Trazodone for a week to see if it would prevent the excessive sleeping. He tried to explain this idea to Mother, but she looked at me and indicated that I should decide. At least she knew I was caring for her.

As the doctor and I discussed Mother's situation, I mentioned my thoughts on her just not waking up. Alzheimer's itself doesn't kill, the doctor said, but something else does: frequently heart failure or choking. He said that the lifespan of an Alzheimer's patient is 2–10 years following diagnosis. Mother had been diagnosed for $3^{1/2}$ years earlier. Knowing her genetic makeup, there was the possibility that she could be with us for a long time. There were two good results today: I knew Mother still cared for me, and Mother knew I was looking out for her.

Time to Throw Out the Birthday Cake

"Hi, Mother. What are you doing?" I said as I approached her in the dining room on an early May visit.

"Just rambling around," she replied.

As we seated ourselves—Mother in her green chair and me in my red, folding chair—I related about talking with my oldest brother and how he was recovering from a cold.

"It's better when everyone cares about others," she commented.

Once again, I had brought her a piece of her birthday cake from January that I still had in the freezer, but today she did not seem interested in it. She kept wanting me to eat it, although I told her I had had a piece earlier. Finally, she allowed me to feed her a couple of bites, but that was all. It was time to throw away the four-month-old birthday cake.

Mother's Day

Mother was surprisingly alert and more agile in May. Could it be the reduced dose of Trazodone the doctor had prescribed? The staff said Mother was up early that day. She was walking much better, too. When quizzed on Mother's Day, she told the staff that her boys would come to visit. I had brought some red roses and blue lilies for her, and a piece of purloined cake from a reception at the church.

Mother seemed more alert. Since her nails were bothering her, I pulled out the nail file to smooth them. She wanted to do it herself. While this act seemed small, it was the first time in many months that Mother had taken on such a role for herself. Conversation centered on the weather and what we had done today. After we agreed on how warm it was, Mother lapsed, saying, "I believe Dan is cold today."

I noticed her breathing becoming heavy, and then she was asleep. As time neared for the Sunday church with Chaplain Mark, I woke Mother.

"Mother, mother," I said gently to wake her.

She awoke with a jerk.

"It's about time for the church service," I said.

Mother had a perplexed look on her face.

"Your church service is about to begin. I will walk with you to the meeting place, but then I need to go," I said, hoping to ease away quietly. "You enjoy the church service," I continued, "and your friends will be there."

Mother, still looking perplexed, said, "Why do I enjoy this?"

We went to the church service. Folks were already gathering, but I found Mother a chair up front across from two ladies who, quite frankly, looked as if they too needed an explanation as to why they enjoyed this activity. I kissed Mother and left her in good spirits. It was a good Mother's Day.

All Those Big Houses

Mother was in the TV room with several other residents on Wednesday in early August. She was sound asleep. I gently woke her, and she asked, "Are we going home now?" I asked her if I could clean her glasses—this act had become our routine. But then she said something surprising: "Clean your glasses first and then clean mine."

Mother remembered that I cleaned my glasses also. This little snippet of conversation told me that she still remembered some things, especially those of her kind character. Her *self* was still in there to some degree, even if her mind was all over the place.

She did not want to walk or go back to her room. She wanted to stay where she was, so we did. Mother seemed content, although some of her later comments made me wonder if she thought the others around her were her family. She was content to be with them.

"I rode around and visited …." Mother allowed.

"Who with? Some relatives?" I asked.

"Lots of folks are here," Mother remarked. "I have been thinking about all their big houses, the ones my family have."

"Have you visited them," I asked, to see where her mind was.

"Just the ones they live in," Mother replied, adding, "I don't know how long they will stay."

She mentioned something about visiting them. Did she think they were her family?

"Danny came about 4 p.m. He hasn't been doing much and is not working," Mother said, reflecting a conversation she and I had had earlier. However, it seemed that the person to whom she was talking was removed from the action. It was not me there in front of her but someone else. Who was I to Mother today? Mother told me that all her family had big houses and that she had visited them over the weekend.

Mother was conversant, happy, and content. She was with family in one way or another, I thought. Maybe she was remembering them, or maybe she was happy just being with folks. I didn't know.

No Big Momma

Mother was wrapped in a blanket over her heavy sweater, sitting in her chair, sound asleep. It was the middle of August. I let her sleep for five or so minutes while I watered her plants and worked the crossword puzzle. Finally, she opened her eyes and saw me.

After chatting briefly and my cleaning her glasses, she mentioned trying to find her room and asked what the name of the place was. I told her and said that she had been here a long time.

"You're the big momma here now," I joked.

Mother replied, "I don't want to be the big momma. Just let me be one of the lower ones." This was truly Mother's *self* speaking.

I had begun to think of my visits with Mother in her world as sacred times. I realized how special they were and knew memories of them would be forever.

I Am Into Ladies' Clothes Now

Three-and-a-half years into Mother's stay in Memory Care, the staff called to say that Mother needed some new clothes. Although the family and I had discussed the need, I had neglected to act. The change in Mother's shape and her need for incontinence pads meant that she required larger pants. At $95^{1/2}$ years old, Mother's upper body had also changed, so she needed larger tops. I knew this, but it took a call from the staff to remind me to buy new clothes. This was not my finest moment—I needed a sister for sure.

The family and I got into action. I did not know about Alfred Dunner until then, but Alfred Dunner carries clothes for older women who are on the larger side. I headed to *Belk* department store. How hard could it be to find Alfred Dunner pants in size 16P? Surely there were other large women with shape issues? I knew that P stood for petite, but it is a mystery to me as to why "petite" is used in this context.

In the ladies' department I asked for the pants by name and was pointed to a number of racks. I was feeling confident, except that I found no Alfred Dunner 16P pants. Most other numbers and letters were there, but no 16P. Luckily, a sales woman came by to ask if I was finding everything alright. Perhaps she saw me fumbling around in ladies wear, repeatedly checking and handling all of the pants. I told her no, I could not find what I was looking for. Without a moment's hesitation the woman pointed to the Alfred Dunner petite section around the corner. Of course! The petite section. How did I not know that? In the petite section, I found every number and color of Alfred Dunner pants one could hope for. I was right. There were many, many other women needing these clothes.

I took my purchases to Mother's place and talked to Judy, who dressed Mother every weekday and who had politely identified the need for new clothes. I explained that I had bought Mother some new clothes and would bring more later. Judy said she would try the new clothes on over time.

It wasn't long before Judy let me know that the 16P pants were too small. Undaunted, I returned to Belk and purchased the same pants in size 18P. Family members also sent purchases from other stores, mostly pants—lots of pants. I asked Judy to give the tighter ones to other ladies in Memory Care, since there seemed to be a free-sharing of clothes there anyway. (We never did discover where Mother got her first pair of blue jeans from!) I kept a few pairs of smaller pants, just in case Mother began to lose weight.

On my next trip to Belk, I took my wife with me. After the pants success, I wanted to buy Alfred Dunner tops—the petite version of course. We found several tops that matched well with the new pants. (I credit my wife with the "matched well" part.) With the sorry state I had let Mother's clothes fall into, I was elated that Mother (and others residents) now had new clothes.

I mentioned the new clothes Mother was wearing on a day I visited. A bit later in our conversation, Mother said she realized she had not thanked me for them. She smiled and added that several of her friends had complimented her, too, which pleased her. I felt relieved that I would not have to struggle with this issue again—but I was wrong.

Dentist Visit

Because Mother's physical health was so good and she had a good chance of making it to a hundred years or more, we thought it best to keep her teeth in as good a shape as possible. This involved three-month appointments to the dentist. In late October I took her to the dentist for a cleaning.

Mother had slowed considerably in the last several weeks. I dreaded the dentist visit: getting Mother out of the home, into the car, and walking into the dental office. As always, the Memory Care staff had her ready to go. She looked dressy in her brown pants, brown top, and colorful sweater. It had begun to rain, so I had a big umbrella ready.

"How did you find me?" Mother asked.

"I know where you are," I replied as I always did.

"I didn't know we were going to the dentist," Mother continued.

I countered with, "I surprised you with this."

As we left the secure doors to Memory Care, Mother was slow to move. She was very cautious of her steps and conscientiously held onto her walker. It was sprinkling rain a bit, so I held the umbrella over the both of us. Her walker veered to the right and required constant redirection. It seemed to veer worse today. We made it out the door and up the ramp to the car, then the fun began.

It had been getting more and more difficult for Mother to get into the front seat of my car. She couldn't remember how to get positioned. The last time, I had instructed her to place her fanny on the seat and push back with her feet to get further up onto the seat. The same instructions this time did not work as well. Mother seemed to have a hard time understanding or carrying out what she was supposed to do. Also, I wondered, were her legs shorter? She did not seem to have the same reach to be able to push back into the car seat. I tried to lift her, but she was still 150 pounds. I found a small toolkit in the car and tried to get her to put her feet on it to boost her a couple more inches, but she had a very hard time lifting her foot and putting it on the kit. Getting both feet on it was almost impossible.

Eventually, with some pushing and lifting, she made it onto the car seat. She was slumped in a heap, but at least she was in the car. Believing what she told me, that she was comfortable (although I couldn't see how), we drove to the dentist.

"Where are we going?" Mother asked.

"To the dentist," I repeated. "To have your teeth cleaned."

The dentist's office personnel had told me to let them know when we arrived so we could use the ramp in back and avoid the steps. Getting Mother out of the car was not so difficult. I helped move her legs to the side, and Mother slipped off the seat and put her feet on the ground. I did have to convince her that the ground was somewhere down there and that she would reach it—eventually—if she just kept scooting forward. We started up the ramp to the back door.

A few steps along, Mother said, "My shoe is untied." Even with as much memory as Mother had lost, she was still aware of things such as her shoe being untied. Some things are still clicking, I thought.

Mother was slow to move down the hallway and into the treatment room and even slower to get positioned in the chair. It was the same scenario as the car, except the dental chair was lower than the car seat. I helped lift Mother's legs onto the reclining chair. She did look more comfortable there than in the car. The hygienist said that Mother did fine but would not let her use the Waterpik as she had the last time.

Back at Memory Care, we walked to Mother's room. Mother sat in her chair and concluded, "Pretty easy trip." Maybe for you, I thought. Next Monday we have to visit the eye doctor.

Rouge and Such

Judy told me that Mother needed more rouge and face powder so Mother could get dressed up in the mornings. "She uses a lot of face powder, so try to get a larger container," Judy instructed. "And get a lighter color than the beige. And she likes to put on rouge."

Oh boy! First, pants and tops; and now, make-up? I did not know all this came with the job. I was determined to do it immediately to get it over with. I picked up the powder and rouge Mother was using and wrote the names down so I could buy the same stuff, except a lighter-colored powder: Maybelline "Dream Wonder" beige for the face powder and NYC "Cheek Glow" for the rouge. I knew a dollar store close by that carried such items, so I went straight there from Mother's place.

In the store I saw a big sign indicating what I was looking for. I was lucky and found the face powders right away, but no Maybelline products were sold there. All the colors I had written down were of no use. Should I find a Maybelline shop? No. I wanted to finish this task now. I picked up four small compacts of L.A. Colors tan—not beige—face powder. I felt successful, even without Maybelline or a larger container.

Rouge was more difficult. I saw reddish stuff that looked like what women put on their cheeks, but I saw no "rouge." I found a clerk and, emphasizing it was for my mother, inquired about it.

"We should have that right over here," the youngish clerk said. "It's not called rouge now but blush. The older ladies probably say rouge." Why did they have to change the word to blush? I actually knew what rouge was. The clerk walked me to the same spot where I had found the face powder and pointed out L.A. Colors powder blush. Of course, NYC "Cheek Glow" was not available either. I bought Mother one package of L.A. Colors blush without a listed color or type.

Done.

Another Milestone, But Not One You Want

This may have been one of Mother's finest hours. When I arrived, she was ready and waiting for me and knew that we were going to see the eye doctor. It was a struggle putting on her heavy black winter coat before we left. She couldn't quite remember how to get her arms into the sleeves, but working at it together, we got her coat on. We could not get the coat buttoned, but that was okay, she said, as she pulled it tightly around herself and said how warm it felt.

Mother struggled mightily to make it up the ramp to the car and then onto the car seat. We used the little tool kit, as we had a few days before, as a booster. After a short struggle to sit and push back, Mother made a sudden swing with her legs and was on the car seat. She was in.

We had to wait a long time to see the doctor—more than an hour. Mother slept some (I think), but she denied it. When we were called back, Mother was up immediately, trudging the best she could, heavy coat and all (she did not want to take her coat off). First came the initial test with a new technician. Then, we had to move to another room where Mother was given the reading test, the dilation procedure, the glaucoma test, and a final check-over by the doctor.

Despite all this moving and testing, Mother never complained. She obeyed all instructions as best she could understand, even with constant nudging of her head and chin for repositions. It was very difficult for her to hear the technicians, and she had a hard time holding her eyelids open. Despite all this, Mother never complained and complied with everything asked of her.

Mother flunked her eye test, though. She could not make out the big "9" or "5" at the top of the eye chart; she could not see the technician's fingers in front of her or see the technician's nose about four inches away. It was obvious, even to me, that Mother was not seeing much at all. The doctor looked through the big lenses, prescribed an antibiotic gel for her eyes, and commented on the good glaucoma readings. He did not say much except that he couldn't believe it had been a year since he had seen her.

I finally asked if Mother had macular degeneration in her good (left) eye. He nodded yes and said it was the same as her right eye. Next, I asked if she even needed to wear her glasses. He indicated no. She could see some at the periphery. Mother remained upright in her chair, ready for the next test, and did not seem to have heard any of the conversation. I received a note certifying that Mother was legally blind.

On our way out, the clerk said we would get a card in the mail to set up another appointment in a year. Although I did not say anything out loud, in my mind I thought that there was really no need. It was sad to think that Mother had reached another milestone—that of being legally blind. But I do not think I had ever seen such will in a person. Mother never complained and did the best she could. During her lengthy ordeal at the eye doctor, she never flinched. Stoic is the word that comes to mind.

Cutting Christmas Trees

A week before Christmas, I brought a Christmas door decoration with me and hung it up facing the outside. We talked about the tree that the garbage collector had brought her before she moved from her home. I also told her about her sons cutting trees from property that was not ours. She smiled at this story—my, my, what a difference a few years make. We would have never admitted that to Mother back then, when we actually did it!

I talked about the crooked Christmas trees that we had to stand in the corner of the room tied up with guy-wires. She smiled at that too, but I do not know if she remembered. I asked her about getting Christmas trees when she was growing up. She perked up when I asked if they cut them from their woods.

"Oh, yes, we cut them, a cedar or pine or whatever was available," Mother allowed.

She was better now. After Mother fell asleep, I read her quarterly report. She had gained four pounds, and her blood pressure was higher—much higher. Her "elopement" risk had also slightly increased from 11 to 12 on a 10–20 scale. Her fall score remained unchanged at 12, also on 10–20 scale. She had had no falls this quarter. In summary, she was alert but confused.

"Some of Them Did Not Like What I Said"

Mother was asleep in her chair when I arrived to visit on the last day of the year. I got out my red folding chair, banged it against the heater accidentally, and woke her. She opened her eyes and smiled. We exchanged greetings, and I sat down.

"Some of them did not like what I said," Mother began.

"Did they say something to you?" I responded, wondering if some sort of confrontation had occurred.

"No, it just seemed that way."

I wondered if someone had been short with Mother or had expressed displeasure. A few days before, she had complained about being ignored. She was very sensitive to such things. Even today, in response to my question of why she was holding her glasses, she asked if it bothered me. It was a sincere question of concern. It might have been that Mother had interpreted a response as disapproval. That just would not do.

"I'm sure you were kind," I said reassuringly.

"I try to be."

Then Mother was quiet, her eyes closed, and she fell back asleep.

Suddenly, there was turmoil! The lady next door, in Effie's old room, was sitting in her wheelchair and calling out something that sounded like "nurse." She called out repeatedly, almost like a rhythm. Then she would stop. Then she would start calling out again. I was pleased that Mother could not hear well—this would drive her crazy.

It was getting close to dinner time. Mother had mentioned earlier about dinner, so I thought she might be hungry and this would ease my departure. I went to find a staff worker to take Mother to the bathroom before we went down to dinner. I could see immediately that the worker's nature was more abrupt than that of most of the other staff members. I wondered, perhaps unfairly, if Mother's earlier comment, "they didn't like what I said," came from this worker.

The worker wasted no time in getting Mother up from her chair and off to the bathroom. Her commands were direct—not harsh, just direct. In the worker's defense, this trip to the bathroom turned out to be challenging. As she directed Mother into the bathroom, another resident appeared at Mother's door and was about to enter until stopped by the worker. While wandering the floor, this resident had heard the rhythmic calls from next door and was apparently trying to get help for the lady.

"You stay outside, Miz G," the worker instructed. "I will be out in a moment."

But Miz G poked her head in again.

"She tries to help," I said to the worker, reflecting on the fact that Miz G walked around with a notebook looking at rooms.

"Yes," the worker replied dryly. "She 'works' here."

The worker's job was not made any easier by the fact that Mother was not really with it. Finally, I heard the washing of hands, a slow and tedious process that had Mother complaining that the wrinkled-up paper towels hurt her hands. This prompted an apology and a look by the worker and me at Mother's hands to see if they hurt or not. Mother said her hands were tender, and the worker promised to have the nurse look at them.

The worker was trying to finish up with Mother and attend to the lady next door. I told the worker I would walk with Mother to the dining room. Mother took her walker and asked which way to go.

The Darling at 96

I tried to build up Mother's upcoming 96th birthday. Sometimes she surprised me with a remembrance of events, so I planted the idea of her upcoming birthday.

"You have a birthday later this month," I told her. "You will be 96 years old."

She thought a minute and responded, "I won't be 96." She sounded emphatic.

"So, how old do you think you are?"

"About 40," Mother guessed.

"You feel about 40, then?"

"Yes."

We left it at that. I didn't know why Mother had chosen 40. Was there something special about that number, or did it just pop into her head? Most ladies that I had heard discuss an earlier life liked the age 25, it seemed. (This was also a mystery to me.)

More folks were available on the Sunday before Mother's actual birthday, which was four days later. I had bought enough cake, punch, ice cream, and snacks so that 15 members of Mother's family and about 28 residents and staff could have a party in the dining room of Memory Care. Someone had brought a beautiful bouquet of cut flowers and an artificial arrangement for Mother's room. For now, though, the flowers adorned the dining room table along with the cake. Some folks brought gifts. Mother was particularly interested in her white cake trimmed with red roses and the big "9" and "6" candles on top. As we were trying to get organized, Mother's fingers wandered into the icing, which she enjoyed until we could get pieces cut.

Two days later on our drive to the dentist, I reminded Mother of the big party as a lead-up to her real birthday and a continuation of the celebration of her 96 years.

"You had a good birthday party Sunday. Do you remember?" I asked.

"No, I can't remember it," Mother replied.

"You had children, grandchildren, and great-grandchildren there. A lot of folks came, and they had a good time. You had a good time too and ate lots of birthday cake," I continued.

Mother smiled.

"Sunday was not your birthday, though. Your birthday is actually on Thursday, two days from today. We just had your party on Sunday because that is when everyone could come. You will be 96 on Thursday. Can you believe that? Did you ever think you would live to be 96?"

"I haven't yet."

Well said, Mother.

I visited her again on her actual birthday, bringing with me a bag filled with lots of practical things for her.

"Do you know how old you are?" I asked.

"I think about 70, but you thought I was about 90-something," she replied, remembering our earlier conversations.

"I know exactly how old you are," I stated boldly. "You are 96."

I pulled a photo out of the bag and showed Mother. It was a picture of all the family, who attended her birthday party the previous Sunday. I knew she could not see well, so I pointed out each person and told her who they were. She held the picture for a long time, looking at it or just holding it. I told her of the legacy she left with all of us. I could tell she knew what I was saying, but she said nothing. She told me I could put the picture up, but she never let go of it; she just held it, staring at it, until she fell asleep still holding the picture.

As Mother slept, nurse Alicia came in with her medicine. Alicia roused Mother and gave her some water and a cup of custard with the medicine. We showed Alicia the picture at Mother's party, and she commented on Mother's busy day. Alicia, turning to leave, said, "She is so sweet. We just love her."

I thought this was a good time to get the bathroom visit over before dinner. A male worker was sent to help; he was very kind and efficient and had Mother out of her chair and into the bathroom quickly. As I sat in Mother's chair waiting, I thought how Mother had accepted all the staff members there: old, young, black, white, male, female. She seemed to appreciate them all, even the male staff who helped her with the most private activities.

As I left Memory Care, Gina and another lady were talking. She volunteered, "We just love your mother. She did not want me to leave her today, so I just sat with her a while." Everybody seemed to love Mother—the darling at 96.

Missed Opportunity

The visit on a Wednesday about four years into Memory care was much the same as a month before. Mother was alert and sitting in her chair with the bedspread pulled over her legs.

"Somebody put me to bed," Mother said.

"I went to Sunday School at the city hall," she said later.

"Some of the old folks fell asleep."

"It felt good when Gladys (a sister-in-law long deceased) brought me some flowers." Mother and I talked about the flowers I had brought the previous Sunday that were beginning to wilt.

"Some folks came and sang for us today," Mother then said.

Wanting to know if this had really happened, I questioned Gina. Groups do come to sing, but today they had a lady talk about gardening and had then watched folks sing on a video. Mother did not seem to remember the gardening lady, unless she was confusing her with Gladys. As we talked, I told Mother I was writing a book.

"What about?" she asked.

"About you," I said. "I am writing about the time you decided to come and live over here near me. Do you remember that time?"

"I sorta do," she said.

Then, she added a little later, "I have not read much about that."

"I will bring some stories over and we will read them together," I said.

"Okay," Mother said, not too excitedly but not dismissively either.

I had planned to do just that, but I did not and eventually missed the opportunity.

I Had Expected This—Again

Mother did not recognize me on a Saturday visit in late March. I could see in her face and eyes that she did not know me.

"Mother, do you know who I am?" I asked.

"No," she said. "I don't know you."

"I am Dan."

She still had a puzzled look, so I said, "I'm Danny, your son."

"No, you're not my Danny," Mother said, almost defiantly. This was the same response as the first time she did not recognize me. She knew Danny—and this person in front of her definitely was not him. A lady was seated next to Mother. She was alert and was talking to Mother. She asked if I knew the lady next to her, pointing to Mother.

"Yes," I said. "I am her son, but she does not recognize me."

Just then, Mother said, "I recognize him now."

It was better after that, but she spoke very little. I said I was going to her room to check her flowers. She said she did not know where her room was.

Déjà Vu, Sort-of-Gardening, and Tomatoes

As I approached the front door of Memory Care on a Saturday in mid-April, I met the daughter of one of the residents I knew. The daughter said she was there every other day.

"How is your mother?" I asked.

Her hesitating response told me things were not so good.

"Mother could not remember that dad had died," she replied. The daughter seemed very concerned about this change in her mother. I could relate.

Mother was seated with three other ladies in the activities room. She had her head down and did not seem as alert as the other three, who recognized me when I approached them. Mother raised her head as I spoke and looked at me. I convinced her to walk back to her room to visit. Otherwise, I feared a four-way conversation, with the three other ladies and me, but without Mother.

I brought my book to read just in case Mother fell asleep, but I was pleasantly surprised today. Conversation started slowly. I asked her if she slept late, if she felt okay, what she had done today, and so forth. She responded to all my questions much as usual: no, yes, nothing much, and so forth. I cleaned her glasses, cleaned mine, then commented on how much better we both could see. Mother mentioned the sunshine right afterwards, so maybe she did see better. I commented on how nice her fingernails looked and that she must had had them done recently. She said no.

Then we hit on something: "Mother, I planted tomatoes in the garden today. You always grew tomatoes at home." I could see a smile coming, and Mother perked up a bit. We engaged in a long, lucid conversation of growing, canning, and using tomatoes. I knew everything she said was true.

Not To Work Is Not Too Good

In mid-April, Mother and I were just visiting. As she sat quietly, I asked, "Mother, what are you thinking about today?"

"Nothing in particular," she replied, as she usually did. I had asked her this question often just to see if she would give me an answer. I mentioned that it was good not to have anything to do some days. Mother disagreed with me.

"No," she said. "People used to working don't want to have nothing to do. Some people think a job with nothing to do is good, but it is not." These words came from a woman used to working. To do nothing was not good. *Self* again.

"Thank You for Taking Me to the Dentist"

Mother was sitting alone in the TV room, dressed and ready to go. She looked as if her hair had been done, and I was told that she had gone to the bathroom.

"Hi, Mother," I said. "We are going to the dentist today."

She looked a little concerned or confused and wanted to know who all was going. (I am the only one who has ever taken her to the dentist.) I helped her up from the chair, and off we went. It was a struggle for her; I could tell she was more feeble. But we talked and laughed as we walked up the incline to the car. I had brought the Camry rather than the Highlander, since the Camry sat lower, and Mother would be able to get onto the seat much easier than before. It was still difficult, though: She could not get quite far enough back onto the seat so that I could swivel her legs into the car.

"I don't feel like I am on the seat," she said.

Although it was very difficult for her, she seemed to gather her might and will together for a last push and got herself in a good position. I helped move her legs into the car, strapped on her seat belt, and we hit the road.

"Just one foot in front of the other," I said lightheartedly as she trudged up the incline to the door. Catching a glimpse of a smile as she agreed, I continued: "Slowly, one step at a time."

The hygienist cleaned Mother's teeth, and this time without any objections.

We repeated the car-entry procedure on the way home. After Mother got in, we were home within a few minutes. The walk back to her place was downhill and easier. I took Mother to her table for dinner, but we were early. She spoke very little, but she did not sleep. I reminded her that she had her teeth cleaned.

"Show me your teeth," I said.

Mother gave me a good look at her cleaned teeth.

Then, revealing her *self*, she said, "Thank you for taking me to the dentist and for taking care of me."

I told her I was pleased to do it. After a short while, I told her I needed to go but that I would see her again soon.

"Thank you for taking care of me. Will the girls take care of me after dinner?" I assured her that the girls would take very good care of her.

Mother Needs a New Bra

Times had changed. After four years in Memory Care, it was no longer Mother but the folks who dressed her in the morning who decided when it was time to buy new clothes. Judy called and said that Mother needed a larger bra.

The problem was not that Mother had put on a lot of weight (she had only gone up a few pounds) but that her weight had shifted. Just a few days earlier, I had also been told that Mother needed a larger size of incontinent underpants.

Mother's shoes were wearing out, too, and she was complaining that they were no longer comfortable. I realized her weight had shifted there too. Her feet were swollen, and her shoes were too small. Judy suggested that I buy shoes with Velcro or zippers rather than laces.

Mother needed to go on a clothes-buying spree, but she could not—that had become my job. Usually, situations such as this one frustrated me, not because I did not want to get Mother what she needed, but because I did not know *what or where* to get what she needed. This time, though, I felt up to the task. I wanted to take this on, and it was a good thing I did!

Putting off the shoes for the time being, I first approached the purchase of a new bra. I was no longer embarrassed at this point in discussing bras with anyone, male or female, clerk or person on the street. With one of Mother's worn-out bras in hand, I went to my local department store. I told the sales clerk that my 96-year-old Mother's bra was too small. I took out Mother's old bra and showed it to her.

After floundering around on what I meant by "too small" (Was it the band? Was it the cup?), the sales clerk showed me a rack displaying 38D bras, which we concluded would probably fit Mother. She also showed me a rack filled with boxed bras that looked more familiar and found one without wires in white.

"I need two," I told her.

"We only have one of this kind in white."

"That doesn't matter. We can choose another color."

We found the same bra in beige and closed the deal. Later, Judy said they fit.

Now it was on to shoes.

Most women I know have a horrible time finding the right shoes, so they try them on at the store first. Since Mother was not able to get out and try on shoes, I was already one step behind. I had checked the size of her old shoes and they were all 8.5 wide. At least I had a start, I thought, but I had to take back the first pair of shoes I bought because the 8.5 was too small.

I tried another shoe store and found they sold Skechers, a brand Judy had advised me to buy. They did not have the zippers or Velcro that had been recommended, but they did have a soft, slip-on shoe. After telling the sales lady about buying bras for my mother and being assured that I could return the shoes, I bought another pair in size 8.5 wide to try on Mother.

Back with Mother again, I fumbled as I tried to get the tight slip-on Skecher over the tarsal area of her swollen foot.

"That shoe is too small!" Mother said with unusual impatience.

I knew I could go no further with her, so I gave up. Then I tried to put her old shoes back on. I unlaced the first shoe as far as I could and still struggled to get it over her swollen foot.

"You are just messing around," Mother said sourly.

"Do you think I am not trying?" I replied.

Finally, I was able to push her old shoe on and lace it up. I returned the shoes to the store and bought another pair of Skechers size 9, and with the discount I was given bought a second pair of the same shoe in beige. They fit! Judy seemed pleased. Mother seemed pleased. I was elated.

"I Know When It's Breakfast"

Mother was in bed, under the covers, and sound asleep when I arrived on a Saturday in May. She was awakened earlier than normal for her Saturday shower, and the workers had allowed her to return to bed to catch up on sleep. I crept into her darkened room, sat in her green chair, and took the opportunity to doze off myself. I doubted I would see Mother today. She was sound asleep.

Suddenly she moved and said she needed to go to the bathroom. She was serious. I found a worker down the hall and hailed her to help. The worker held Mother up by her arm and said, "Okay, okay. Just get your feet under you so you don't fall." Mother groggily took her walker and made her way to the bathroom.

"Can I go back to bed?" Mother asked when she had finished.

"No," the worker replied. "You have a visitor."

"What?" Mother asked.

"Someone is here to see you. Don't you want to go and find out?"

"Can I go back to bed?" Mother asked again.

"You have a visitor. Don't you want to go and see him?"

"Is it my brother? My son?" Mother asked.

I walked over to her as she exited the bathroom, and called her name and gave her a hug. She knew me right away and no longer wanted to go back to bed.

"Are you getting ready for dinner?" I asked.

"Breakfast," Mother said knowingly.

"You had a long nap this afternoon. So, they will be having dinner," I said.

"Breakfast," Mother repeated a bit more forcefully this time. She knew which meal she ate when she got up … in the morning.

I could see I was getting nowhere with this discussion, so I dropped it.

We talked about coffee, trying to find some common ground.

"I don't like coffee," Mother said. I knew this was a bald-faced lie because she drank coffee every morning, but I let that pass, too. I realized she meant something else, possibly that she did not want coffee *now*.

The worker came in with fresh ice and said something about dinner being in a few minutes. Mother told her she thought it was breakfast. The worker told her she had slept this afternoon and the meal would be dinner.

"Well, if it's dinner, I'll eat dinner," Mother said, cheerfully agreeing. I told the worker we would be down to the dining room shortly. Mother paused for a moment then added, "I sure would like a cup of coffee with my breakfast."

Mother Was Cranky Today

A visit about a month later started pleasantly enough. Mother was in the dining room, so I went first to her room and put her fresh roses in the vase. When I returned, she was a little contrary. First, she insisted that I **not** go and get a tissue to clean her glasses. She flatly refused to let me leave. An old black-and-white movie was on the television, and Mother was watching it.

"Is that Dan and his brother standing up there?" she asked.

I explained to her that the movie had boys playing football, but I had no idea if she could actually see any of the actors or if she was thinking about something else. We sat without talking for a while.

"Mother and Grandmother are real quiet over there," Mother said.

Two ladies were seated at their places at the table. They were not talking, and I wondered if Mother thought they were her mother and grandmother. She had not mentioned her grandmother in recent years. As we sat quietly, Mother allowed that family had visited today, but she had not seen them yet. I was not clear on who she meant. She tried to tell me it was a "relation and their family," but she could not come up with the name, although she tried.

"Awww," Mother said, as she often did when she was annoyed with herself, "they were …" She trailed off, and we left the issue unresolved.

Everyone was gathering early for dinner this day. The ladies had their purple bibs on. I tried to get Mother to let me put hers on, but for the second time today she was being contrary and refused. She then asked about tea and said she needed something to eat with. I pointed out her spoon. Soon the staff brought the drinks: tea and water. She drank some, then picked her fork up and made motions like she was scooping up food. I told her that the food was being prepared and would be brought out soon. I put the purple bib around her neck.

"That sure feels good," she said. It would have felt good earlier, when you were cold, if you had let me put it on then, I thought, but I said nothing.

Another lady sat in her wheelchair at the dining table. Space for feet was tight, but Mother's next comment was surprising. As her feet touched the other lady's under the table, Mother asked, "Is that your daddy's foot?" I explained it belonged to the other lady. When their feet touched again, Mother said angrily, "I despise having someone's foot under me!"

I asked the other lady if I could move her wheelchair over to give everyone more room. Although she showed some hurt feelings after Mother's outburst, she kindly let me move her wheelchair. I told Mother I would see her again soon, kissed her forehead, and left. I thought about Mother and her contrariness as I drove away and hoped that her attitude was not changing to being cranky.

At the intersection, I thought I would never get through; cars were stopping even though they did *not* have a stop sign, and the lady turning left would not go when she had a chance. Finally, out of pure frustration, I darted across the intersection in front of the stranded lady. "I despise it when someone's foot is under me," I thought.

How to Leave Mother Now

On a visit in June the nurse told me that state regulations now required all visitors to be out of the building before the staff began dinner preparations so that staff would not be disrupted by letting people out the security door. The nurse was very nice about it, saying that he hated even to mention it. I told him that I understood.

As I left, I talked to Gina a bit on my way out. She said my older brother had had a rough time Monday, with Mother not showing any interest in his visit until he was about to leave. Gina then said—as we all suspected—that Mother did not remember our visits almost as soon as we left. Gina thought it best to find a way to ease out of Mother's view for a while and then leave, rather than telling her and making any ado about leaving. She thought it would have been best for my brother, when he left to go to Mother's room to bring back peppermints, to have simply left for home at that time.

So, with Mother's state, new rules and Gina's advice, I determined that my visits would avoid mealtimes and be shorter. My leaving would be subtle and quick.

Mother's Problem, My Problem, No Problem

"I can't get out. They keep me locked up, like we are prisoners," Mother lamented.

This was the first time I'd heard this from Mother. It was on a Sunday visit in early August. I didn't say anything, waiting for more information. She wanted to walk some more, and as we did, we crossed paths with a very kind, efficient male worker that I knew well.

"He's one of the bad ones," Mother said. This was strange, but fit with the pattern today. After walking, Mother sat sadly in her chair. She said nothing at first, but her expression was one of hopelessness, of not knowing what to do. She was anxious.

"I hope Dan can be alright."

"Is he sick?" I asked, playing along.

"Nooo," Mother responded, "he's got something that he doesn't know how to do. Maybe he can work it out. I will try to help him."

"I will try to," I added.

"Just have to work things out the best you can," Mother added, before falling into a restless sleep. (She had transferred her feeling of despair onto me—I was now the one with the problem, not her.)

Suddenly, Mother woke with eyes wide open. "We have to help Mildy," she exclaimed.

"Where is Mildy?" I asked.

"In with Audie. She will be here a while but not stay much longer. Audie is alright to stay by herself."

"Has Audie been sick?" I asked.

"Yeah, yeah."

"Get back to stay with Mildred. She is very lonely and all."

I may have misunderstood, but it made more sense that Mother was talking about Mildred and not Mildy. Mildred was Audie's sister, and they needed help—my help … or Mother's help. Mother then said she thought I was helping the others and Mildred to get along today. She expressed the need for us, mainly me, to help our folks who stay by themselves.

"Mildred will soon get to running her own life, maybe," Mother said. "It's getting pretty late, so you can loosen and do what you need to do." She then went silent and stared off into a corner.

"What are you thinking about?" I asked.

"Nothing in particular," Mother replied.

I tried to talk about something else. I told her about my oldest granddaughter, and mentioned that this was her great-granddaughter. Mother smiled. I told her that my granddaughter would begin high school this week. "She is anxious a bit," I said.

"The unknown," Mother said knowingly.

"Exactly," I said. "The unknown."

Mother then said, "Don't worry about me."

Trying to lighten up the day, I offered, "It is okay to think about you, isn't it?"

Mother smiled and said, "You can think about me. Yeah, think about everybody."

"I hope Mildred will be okay," I replied. "I hope she gets better."

"Have to help each other through times."

"We always have," I said.

"Yeah," Mother added.

"We'll get over, and you and Mildred can talk about what you need to. I won't have much to say."

"This had been something that Minkey found and she has dealt with it pretty well," replied Mother, using Mildred's nickname for the first time in a while.

Mother seemed to settle a bit. We talked about supper, then I told her I needed to check with the office and would be right back.

I found the goodhearted weekend nurse in the office and asked about Mother. She indicated that Mother had been anxious, adding, "They [the residents] get together and talk about things and get the same ideas." I asked about *escaping*. The nurse laughed and said, yes, they talk about things like that. I mentioned another lady who had always wanted to escape. The nurse laughed again and agreed.

Perhaps the mystery of Mother being a "wanna-be escapee" was triggered by the others talking about wanting to "get out." As I puzzled over this day, some thoughts emerged. Was it possible that being cooped up had led Mother and the other residents to believe they were being held against their will? Had Mother got caught up in it? There was no way for her to deal with this—at least initially—but she eventually seemed to work it out. She had found a way forward. Not just the being cooped up, but the problem of the "unknown." Two days later, the problem had evaporated.

Time for the Wheelchair

Mother (almost) never complained; she was always okay. That was until a Saturday in early August when she volunteered that her left knee was hurting badly. As I checked on her toiletries, I noticed a wheelchair in the corner of her room. I was surprised I had not noticed it before, considering how small Mother's room was.

"Have you been in a wheelchair today?" I asked. Her answer, as often was the case, was not a clear yes or no.

"Mother, I thought it would be good to use a wheelchair next time we go to the dentist. We don't have to go back for a while, but next time."

I brought this up, fearing how she might respond. Although her answer was unclear, it was obvious that she would not object. It was also obvious that she had used the chair before. The rules indicated that Mother could not stay in Memory Care if she was not ambulatory, but a wheelchair counted as ambulatory. I stopped by the Medicare equipment supplier and got the skinny on Medicare paying for wheelchairs.

At my next visit, Mother said her knee did not hurt and that she "was beyond that now"—of course, she had no pain because she was seated and had been transported around in a wheelchair. Later that same week, Mother walked from the dining room to her room; she was hard to keep down! The next time she tried to walk, the staff put her in the wheelchair. The anti-inflammatory medicine her doctor had prescribed was working, and she had less pain and wanted to walk. However, it was clear that the staff wanted Mother to use the wheelchair.

Good Relations

On a Saturday visit in mid-August Mother was sitting in a wheelchair at her place in the dining room next to a neighbor who was also in a wheelchair. Mother was awake. She smiled and said it was good to see me. I asked about her knee, but I am not sure she remembered that it had hurt her.

"What are you thinking about?" I asked.

Rather than the usual "nothing much," this time Mother said that she was thinking about … then she paused and asked me what we were talking about yesterday. Since the conversation was back to me, I had to come up with something to move it forward. After a moment, I said that I thought we were talking about the weather. I figured the weather was a safe bet. Mother shook her head and said, "No, but something similar."

"Well, you looked like you were intently thinking about something. You know how people look when they are intently thinking about something," I said.

"I guess I was thinking about what I was intently thinking about," Mother said. Then she laughed and I laughed, and we both enjoyed her good nature.

Judy came around and spoke softly to Mother. The topic of work came up, and Judy said to Mother, "I bet you were a hard worker."

Mother smiled and said she thought Judy was a hard worker. I put in that she was.

"She is a good social worker," Mother said about Judy, suggesting for the second time today that she was more aware of her surroundings than I had realized.

Today, I went to see Mother, fearing what I would find. Instead, I found the best conversation we had had in a while. As I prepared to leave, I kissed her on the forehead, and she kissed my cheek. I said I would see her again soon.

"I hate for you to leave," Mother said.

All the Help We Can Get

As the latter part of August rolled around, Mother was pretty much full-time in her loaner wheelchair. The staff worried about her getting up and trying to walk.

My next mission was to get Mother her own wheelchair, which is straightforward if one avoids the pitfalls and maintains proper communication with the nurse and doctor. Once the nurse and I got our wires straight about who was doing what, the very efficient nurse took the process forward, and Mother had a new 18-inch wheelchair in just a day or so. Mother began to push herself backwards in the wheelchair within a few days. I do not recall any concerns or issues with her and the wheelchair. We hoped she had learned enough not to slip out of the wheelchair onto the floor, as she had done with the loaner wheelchair a few days earlier.

With the wheelchair issue now sorted out, I began the search for lift chairs—a recliner that "lifts up" to allow the person sitting to get to their feet easily. Lift chairs were expensive and not easy to find, so I had to make a lot of calls. I finally found a store that had a dark-brown vinyl lift chair with a remote and included a four-year warranty on the chair and electrics. I noticed that the reclined position actually raised the legs slightly higher than the body, which would be perfect for Mother and her swollen legs. My wife approved the look of the chair—ensuring that I did not buy a cheap-looking vinyl chair and thereby embarrass my brothers.

The store guys delivered the new lift chair to Mother's room that afternoon, plugged it in, tried it out, and then we all left. Mother was already seated for dinner and was not involved. As I left through the security doors with the store guys, I told the nurse that the lift chair was in but Mother did not know anything about it. The nurse replied, "That is probably good."

Mother Is Learning To Drive

I found Mother moving herself in her wheelchair in the hallway outside her room in late August. The staff said she had been rolling all over the floor that day. They also said that she got up and walked twice, but they cautioned her not to do that. Mother used the outer wheel rim to propel herself rather than using her feet. I noticed she already had a red mark on her hand from pushing with the rim. I hoped she would use her feet soon. I asked if I could push her somewhere.

"No, I do not want to go that way. No, I do not want to go the dining room. I thought you were going in there. You should not be going over that mountain. Let's go right, no left." She could not decide where she wanted to go, and wherever I chose was not where she wanted to be. Finally, we wound up in her room.

"Have you sat in your new chair?" I asked proudly.

"That's the teacher's chair," Mother said.

"That's *your* chair," I emphasized to her.

"My chair?"

We agreed the chair looked nice, but Mother had nothing more to do with it. I was a little disappointed. The next day she asked why I had gotten a new chair. What was wrong with the old one? I sat in Mother's new chair while she continued to roll around in her wheelchair. While I was sitting in the new chair, Mother managed to roll over my feet and get caught on another chair, but she would not stop moving. I stayed in her chair while she "practiced driving" in the hallway. I overheard her talking to her neighbor next door as the neighbor sat in *her* wheelchair. Perhaps seeing so many others in their wheelchairs made Mother fit in. Maybe it was like her first walker, when she quickly chose one just like all the other ladies had.

As the nurse walked me out, she said that Mother was doing well and had been all over the hallway in her wheelchair that day. That was good news. The other bit of good news was that Mother was now considered ambulatory. For the time being, we did not have to worry about another move.

Mother Is One of Them

Mother had just finished getting her nails filed and polished when I arrived. She sat dutifully in her wheelchair with her hands stretched out over a paper towel, letting the nails dry. After her nails had dried, I wanted to take Mother back to her room to talk. I detected a little hesitation to leave.

I sat in her new lift chair, and Mother was next to me in her wheelchair. She seemed to be slumped in the chair, and I wondered if she would do that more and more. As she sat there, Mother continuously fiddled with her nails, biting them and gnawing at the polish. "I have this sticky stuff all over," she complained as she fiddled. Wanting to change the conversation, I asked, "Do you want to go the dining room and see what's going on there?"

Mother responded, "Well, you're the one who wanted to come *here*."

It was clear that Mother was happier sitting with the other ladies than sitting with me in her room. She seemed particularly pleased to be with her neighbor at their table during the day. I told Mother I needed to go and run some errands and then left. She was not clingy but told me to come anytime.

No Reality, None, Nada

Mother was sitting in her wheelchair outside the office on a mid-September Saturday. As I arrived and passed by the office, the male worker volunteered: "She has been helping today." I interpreted that to mean it had been a difficult day. Mother was not herself.

"Do you want to go to your room to visit?" I began.

"No, no, I don't want to go back there," she stated emphatically.

"Do you want to go to the dining room?"

"No, I want to stay right here."

Mother was insistent. She did not want to move to anywhere else. She kept watching the staff in the office and making comments. "I don't know why they just don't finish up," Mother decried. "They just don't know how to do their job."

"They have to get the houses fixed up so they can get some rent," she offered later, her comments laced with references to a deceased first cousin, her boys, Dad (or "your Dad," as she said), and other family members. She was anxious and a bit contrary.

"I am not anxious," she said at one point shortly after having said she was anxious. "It's hard you know. You would think so too if you had to do this," Mother said without indicating what was hard.

"It's night. They should finish up. We should be on our way home."

"Well," I said, "There is a little daylight left. It's four o'clock."

"It's night," Mother repeated with conviction. "You know it's nighttime."

"It's four in the afternoon," I repeated. "Look, see my watch," I stupidly said, forgetting for a moment she could not see and forgetting that I should not challenge her. I had forgotten fantasy validation therapy. She stubbornly held to her view that "it was nighttime, and the people should finish up and just go home." She moved from a contrary to a downright feisty, critical mood. I tried to reason with her. "Mother," I began again, "are you waiting for them to do something for you? Is that why you are waiting here?"

"No, I am not waiting for anything," Mother replied. "You know, they have to get the roof fixed and … (she could not get her words out) so they can get some rent." She avoided my question and went back to the source of her anxiety—the fact that the job was not done and she could not go home.

"Well, you know they have to get everything … fixed up so they can get some rent."

"Look, there goes someone else in there," Mother said, motioning to the office.

"Mother," I began, "that is just the office where they work. They are not going to finish and leave. They will be here all night. They are doing their job, which is to take care of you and others."

Mother then said she was not concerned about anything and everything was all right.

"Look, they are gathering for supper," I said. "Do you want me to take you to supper?"

She perked up a bit and gave me some hope when she said, "Supper? Are they going to fix it?"

"They are fixing supper now for you and the others," I said.

"Not for me," Mother said. "I have food at home."

A staff member said that Mother had been anxious all day, while another worker said she had been like that all week. She was not causing any problems but was just anxious and upset. I told the worker I was going to leave because I could do nothing. I was upsetting her with my questions, and she was upsetting me with her answers. The workers said they would get her to supper and try to distract her. Mother was completely detached from reality today.

When I returned home and my wife asked about Mother, I told her the saga. "What about a urinary tract infection?" she asked.

Picking Beans and Being Snippy

I visited Mother a few times in her unreal state. She was calmer, though, and we had a good conversation. She was wrapped in a blanket and sitting in her wheelchair next to Betsy in the TV room. She smiled and said hello. I told her I had fertilized my yard that morning. She told me she had fertilized her yard a few days ago. I told her I had picked some green beans that day. She told me she had picked some of her beans a few days ago. It was a good conversation, although she seemed slower. She did not hurt anywhere, but she did not seem happy. A UTI test had not been done.

The nurse related that Mother had been "snippy" of late. Sometimes she was her sweet old self, and suddenly she would become snippy. For example, when a worker tried to place Mother's hand on a rail, Mother told the worker not to touch her. Everyone thought this strange—I did too. The nurse went on to say Mother had shown this attitude several times lately but then reverted to being sweet and kind. He said Mother was going downhill quickly—both physically and mentally.

Wise Sayings Still

"Thanks for coming over here and speaking to me," Mother said on my visit in early September. This was a strange thing for Mother to say, so I asked her if she knew who I was.

"I can't place you now," she said.

"I'm Dan, your son," I told her.

"Oh yeah. I recognize your voice," she then said.

I told her about a saying I had recently heard when I was trying to get things done: "You have to do something before you can do something."

Mother smiled broadly and added, "That is right when you are your own boss."

At face value, she was exactly right. If you are your own boss, it does seems like there are a thousand things to do before you can do the one thing that really needs to be done. You always have to do something before you can do something else. I am sure Mother knew that.

The other advice she gave that day came after I told her about my 50th high school class reunion and how I was a little depressed when it was over. Mother advised, "You have to remember and then let it go."

"Just Live"

Mother was asleep in her chair on a mid-December Wednesday. I sat next to her and did some figuring, waiting for her to wake. Finally, she did.

"It's kind of you to visit me," Mother said. Her comment caught me a little off guard. It was different from the times when she asked how I had found her, or if I had just come by, or something else. She was not anxious but sedate and reconciled to her status. I told Mother that my wife and I were going over to Emory University Hospital the next day. Mother immediately looked at me with concern, wanting to know what was going on. I said it was just a follow-up visit for my wife.

Mother offered one of her maxims: "No need to fret about it. Just live the best we can." As she sat quietly looking straight ahead, I asked her what she was thinking about. "My mind is just zipping around," she said with a smile. Then later she allowed, "It's good that someone penned up can enjoy a visit."

That summed up her attitude today.

Another New Year

Mother was as alert and bright as I had seen her in some time. I told her it was New Year's Day. Mother had a white glove on her left hand, one that she had gotten for Christmas. I did not ask about the right one. I removed her previous year's calendar and pulled out the new one I had gotten a few weeks earlier. Again, it was a free one from our bank. Last year I doubted I would be looking at another January in Mother's room.

I put all her Christmas decorations in two boxes and set them aside to take back home. I took the stocking I had hung from her door and placed it in one of the boxes, collected her three Christmas cards to toss in the recycle bin, and told her I would store the decorations for her until next Christmas. It did not take long to put Mother's room back as it had been before Christmas.

"There's not much for you to do," Mother said.

"No, not much to do today," I agreed.

"Just hold it open," she said.

I was not sure what she meant, but she could have meant to just open the store in case there was any business—unlikely as it might be. I remembered things like that from Dad's business days. I told Mother she had a birthday coming up in January.

"January 29th," Mother said with a grin.

I asked her if she knew how old she would be. She thought a moment but said she could not come up with that.

I offered, "97."

"Audie is older," Mother said.

I told her that I had a birthday in January too. Mother said I would be older. I guessed she thought that I was Aubrie. Then she said that Audie had told her to get into her bed (meaning the reclining chair). Audie was *still* looking after Mother, or so it seemed. Soon, Mother's eyes were drooping. She dozed and then woke.

"Are you comfortable?" she asked.

"Yes, I'm comfortable."

She dozed, awoke, dozed again, and awoke again.

I said, gently chiding her, "You can't stay awake."

"That's what you can do when there is nothing else to do," Mother said with some clarity. "Can you see okay?"

I thought then that I would not be surprised to be putting out her Christmas ornaments again and turning the calendar to next year's January.

Five Years and Running

On March 1, Mother had been in Memory Care for five years. She was asleep in her lift chair, wrapped in her gray fleece blanket when I walked into her room. I put her bags of personal supplies on the shelf, retrieved my red chair, and waited for her to wake up.

"How are you doing, Mother?" I began as usual.

"I don't feel very well," Mother uncharacteristically replied. Several questions later I still did not know why she did not feel well. She said it had started the day before. She was very sleepy today, as she had been for the last several weeks. I held her hand.

"Your hands are warm," Mother said, smiling as if it pleased her. I asked if she was warm. She said she was and commented on having Mildred's blanket on her.

"Mildred will need her blanket when she comes back," Mother said. I said we would find another blanket, and we did not discuss this issue any more.

"I don't know what makes Mildred have these sick spells," she continued, "You'll need some supper."

Mother drifted off to sleep again, then woke and complained that her left knee hurt. I raised her lift chair a little. She repeated that she did not feel good, then fell asleep. Mother slept, and I worked on my crossword puzzle. A worker came to take her to the bathroom and then to lunch.

"I'm not getting up," Mother firmly asserted to her.

I began my departure at that time, telling Mother I would see her again soon and that the worker was there to take care of her and get her to lunch. Mother had a defiant, puzzled look on her face as the worker began the process of convincing Mother of what she was, in fact, going to do. The worker, although slight of frame, was just as determined as Mother. I left thinking that the staff was earning their pay today.

Hospice?

Nurse Alicia had indicated to my brother that Mother might be ready for home hospice care. She was concerned that Mother was not able to feed herself, among other issues. I visited Mother on Friday to see her, to bring more Depends, and to talk with Alicia about hospice. Mother was having a pretty good day. She was asleep when I approached her in the dining room, sitting in her chair at her place, but she woke when I came over.

"I almost was asleep," she said. "But you woke me."

The daytime nurse when Mother first moved into Memory Care now worked next door in Personal Care. She saw Mother and came over to have a word. The nurse bent down and hugged on Mother, saying something to the effect that she herself was good, but maybe not as good as the worker now taking care of Mother. "But let's not tell her that," the nurse jokingly told Mother.

Mother then said, "I don't think you have to take a backseat to anyone. But we will keep that between us." I thought Mother held the conversation together better than I had seen her do in a long time. She was engaged, remembered the two points of the conversation, and responded appropriately. Earlier she had remembered that April 1 was April Fool's Day.

After a while, Mother fell asleep again, and I left to talk to Nurse Alicia. Alicia repeated that it might be time for hospice care and explained that while most folks think of hospice as providing care for the last few days, it can last much longer. She went on to talk about more care so Mother would not have to move out. I agreed that that was our goal. She then said she would call for a time to meet with us to discuss the issue of hospice and Mother. She did not know about Medicare paying for it.

Back home, a quick internet search showed that Medicare would pay for home hospice (even in a nursing home) if the patient had six months or less to live and the decision was made not to cure but only to make comfortable. The six-month time frame was also subject to multiple extensions.

Wanting to Go Home—Again

"I'm waiting for Dad," Mother said when I approached her in the activities room on a Thursday in late May. Then she added: "It's the first time I've been over here. Danny is here. He came first. They dropped me off. I came with this lady who wanted to come to the meeting."

I had come today because Gina said Mother was back to wanting to go home every day in the afternoon, and often waited for Dad or someone to pick her up. (Dad seemed to be more prominent in Mother's mind now than he had been a while back.) With all the talk about going home, I told Mother that her old house needed repairs and that she had moved here. Home was here now, and she was happy.

Mother replied, "I did not mean that I was not happy."

"I know. I just wanted you to know that you do not have to go anywhere."

But later, Mother said again, "It's getting dark. We need to go home." I asked one of the staff members if she was ready to take Mother to supper. Not just yet, she responded, with a look that indicated Mother had worn the staff out this day.

Mother Was Ready to Talk

Mother was just waking from a good nap in the TV room. She was perky, knowing me right away. She was 180 degrees different from a few days back when she was lethargic and weak. She was ready to talk today, and the subject was … *work*. I told her about getting our house painted.

She started tentatively, "I was … (there was a long pause as she searched for a word) typing and … (another long pause) finished what I had to do. They interviewed me."

It was not a straightforward discourse by Mother, but the essence was some sort of work she was given to do. She mentioned typing, being reviewed, the school's work, part-time employment, the lunch provided, people needing to work, work helping people, and so on. She seemed to be talking about office work but then shifted to something else.

"You learn to make up your bed the way they want you to," she added.

Maybe this was where the food for part-time workers came in. Mother talked continuously—haltingly but continuously—for several minutes. She was engaged and telling me a situation. Other than getting some words wrong and not being able to come up with others, Mother talked with minimal interjections by me until she had finished. Then she was silent.

I did not know if she was remembering a time past, an interview, a part-time job, or whether it was all made up. I did not recall Mother ever having an office job or doing any typing for anyone. It could have been a school class where she typed and the instructor checked it over. It was too bad that bits were missing, and I could not get the entire story today.

Lunch was called. A worker was there to take her to the dining room. I said goodbye and that I would see her again. She fussed just a little that I was leaving. Then, alert and in a clear voice, she said, "Goodbye, Dan."

Forgetting a Little Bit at a Time

Toward the end of June of her fifth year in Memory Care, Mother declined further mentally. Our conversations were even less than they had been a few weeks earlier. She did not seem to recognize me on one Wednesday visit, as indicated by her distant look and never calling my name.

On Saturday, with Mother showing the same look as the last visit, I asked her, "Mother, do you know who I am?"

"No, I don't think I do," she answered.

"I am Dan." After no response I continued, "I am your son Dan."

Mother still did not say anything. There was no argument, such as "No, you are not my Dan," as she had once said. It seemed that today she did not even know there was a Dan. I mentioned the previous visits of my brothers, just to see her response. She did not say much of anything. Although Mother did not respond to Dan, she still knew she had three sons. She mentioned that Audie had on long sleeves today, seeing a staff worker with long sleeves. But mostly, we sat silent.

On my way out the secure door, I asked a worker about Mother. She indicated that Mother perked up when "Danny" was mentioned. I did not know how far back the worker referred to, but today that had not been the case. Mother seemed to be forgetting more of us. She looked and acted more like an Alzheimer's patient today. The worker said that Mother showed irritation with staff trying to move her in a direction she did not want to go.

In early July, Mother again did not know me. She had a look in her eye that indicated so, and when asked said she didn't know who I was. I listed the names of her three sons, but she did not seem to remember them. Our conversations were just as empty as those we'd had when she did know me. Mother fell asleep and slept hard. When she awoke, her eyes were different and she recognized me again, saying I did not sound like Dan earlier. We suspected that Mother knew us by our voices but not by sight. It seemed as though she was forgetting us a little bit at a time. She did not know, and then she did.

I Am Into Larger Women's Clothing Now

Judy had said to stay away from the petite section when I next shopped because Mother now needed larger sizes. In addition, the arduous task of buying her new shoes not long back had proved inadequate as her shoes were again too tight and hurting her feet.

I was told that Mother required size 20P pants and 2X blouses—and I should get pull-up pants with an elastic waistband. Okay, I thought, and off to Belk I went, again looking for Alfred Dunner. But salvation was not to be had this time. I could not find size 20P anywhere. I even wandered into the regular Alfred Dunner section hoping to find something. There were no size 20s to be found, and there were no kind ladies to point me in the right direction.

I improvised. I found a denim-looking material with an elastic waist in the size 18W–22W. That was larger at least, I thought, and might work. I bought one pair and grabbed a 2X blouse on my way to the checkout. I was okay with the blouse, but the 18W–22W pants were sort of ... tent-like. The staff used the expression "way too big," but Mother had them on the next day with the legs rolled up a layer or two. Staff said they could do something with the pants, but I was not sure what.

Nurse Alicia reiterated that I should go to Walmart and get 20P pants with an elastic top. However, even at Walmart I did not find straight 20P pants, but instead 18W–20WP knit pants with an elastic top. In the meantime, I had learned that the P meant the pants legs were short. I bought Mother a pair of black Walmart knit pants and was told they fit, so I returned to buy two more pairs in black and brown. I found a white 2X blouse to go with the pants. I was pleased to see Mother in her brown pants and white blouse the next day.

Shoes, Shoes Everywhere But Nary a Shoe That Fits

In addition to buying clothes, I also had to get Mother new shoes—which I had tried in vain to do many times. I had previously bought shoes, only to return them, and now I lacked another shoe plan. Where would I find shoes that did not hurt Mother's feet?

I was thinking ... maybe just socks? At one time Mother had owned a pair of very nice sandals that did not pinch her feet. Another time she had worn a pair of pink, sock-like bedroom slippers. She also wore her Walmart bedroom shoes I bought earlier and her worn, black lace-ups.

I asked about Mother's shoes, really just trying to find out where the shoes came from. I was told that a weekend worker—someone whom I had never seen or heard of—was getting shoes for Mother. I knew no more than this.

Not wanting to let failure be the final word in buying Mother some shoes, I saw an advertisement in the Sunday newspaper that led me toward "cardigan slippers." Needing to purchase two pairs to qualify for free shipping and handling, I bought both large (size 8–9) *and* extra-large (size 8.5–10) slippers. Surely, I thought, one of these sizes would fit.

When they arrived, the slippers looked small—even the extra-large pair. I took both pairs over to the ladies who dress Mother in the mornings and left them. I tried to explain to Nurse Alicia my latest plan. Alicia listened patiently, then said, "I think you are okay with the shoes. You don't need to do anything else."

She said this not knowing if my latest effort would pay off. I was pleased, however, to see Mother wearing the extra-large cardigan slippers a day or so later. The large pair was stashed in Mother's top dresser drawer. Not wanting to return them, I asked Alicia to give the large pair to someone else there who could wear them. The good news was that Mother now had foot coverings; the better news was that I had been relieved of shoe duty.

"I Am Not That Much Out of It"

I was away a good bit of the summer, spending three weeks in Alaska in July and then traveling to the beach in August. I did not see Mother as often as before, but in late August and September, I tried to visit her more often. The conversations were limited. On a Saturday visit in early September, she looked particularly out of it. I did not think she knew me by her expression.

"Mother, do you know who I am?" I finally asked.

"I don't believe I do," she replied. I was expecting this answer from her countenance—I was over any disappointment that my mother did not know me. My brother, though, was not. In August, for the first time, Mother did not know him. And the surprises from her kept coming. When I visited Mother on the following Monday and again two days later, she did not seem very alert.

"Mother, do you know who I am?" I asked again, as I had two days earlier.

"I think you are Danny," she said softly. Then she added, "I am not that much out of it."

Is It Time for Hospice Care?

During the later months, Mother seemed to decline further. By December, she was pretty much wheelchair-bound and slept 90 percent of the time, according to the nurses. On a mid-December visit, I noticed how uncomfortable she seemed to be, moving around in her wheelchair to ease the tension. Her legs were wrapped in bandages because sores had developed on her swollen legs.

A few days later, the doctor thought it was time to have Mother assessed to enter in-house hospice care. I had to choose one of three companies in the area that provided hospice care.

I already knew that a patient had to have an expected life span of six months or less to be considered, so I was not too surprised that the doctor would consider hospice care now. I chose the service connected to the hospital that owned the retirement center—I thought it might make things simpler in case Mother had to go to the onsite hospice building just up the hill. A brother and I met near the end of December to finalize hospice care plans for Mother.

I did not have any mixed feelings on this decision. Mother had been so uncomfortable during the last visit that I was pleased some more care could be given to her. I wondered how close we were to those "six months."

"I Wish You Would Get Out of My Plate!"

Mother was wheelchair-bound now. She seldom got out of the chair, and she recently complained about her legs hurting when she stood. As we were sitting in her room after I had put away her Christmas decorations, I noticed her swollen, blue hand. I asked her if it hurt.

"Just my finger," Mother said, still angry with me.

Earlier I had noticed she was pulling at her nail, and I offered to cut it down a bit. Since I was in charge of fingernails now, I had brought a pair of nail clippers with me. We agreed I should clip the nail. As I tried to work the cutting part under her nail, I found it difficult to separate out a part of the fingernail to clip. Finally, I thought I had a clear shot at the nail. So, I clipped.

"Owww!" Mother said in a loud, angry voice. "You cut me. Why did you do that?"

I looked hard but saw no blood and really no evidence I had cut her. My story is that I did not. Regardless, though, Mother felt pain and let me know about it. I admit to not doing a bang-up job of clipping her nail, but I wondered if she was overly sensitive to pain now. Nevertheless, she was unhappy with me—it was as though she thought I had done it on purpose.

As angry as Mother was with me, her rebuke was perhaps not as bad as the one she had recently given Nurse Alicia. Mother was having trouble getting her food on her spoon to feed herself, so Alicia fetched another spoon and was using it to scoop food onto Mother's spoon. After a while, Mother said pointedly, "I wish you would get out of my plate!"

Mother was not feeling well with her swollen legs and hand. I wondered if Mother was tiring of it all.

Failing To Get Into Hospice

We met the hospice care folks at the appointed time, but the upshot was that Mother did not yet meet all of the criteria required to enter the program. She was close, but could still feed herself and carry on something resembling a conversation. Expectations were that she would be admitted if she developed any other problems. The swelling of her legs and the incumbent sores were of concern but were not enough to put her under hospice care.

The doctor had said if Mother was not accepted into hospice care, that he would order some new tests and write a prescription for home health care. She would now receive extra care for her legs, as well as other assistance. We would also get an update on her health and maybe learn the cause of Mother's leg swelling.

Starting the New Year With A Bang

No matter what the family did for New Year, Mother outdid us all! At 3:15 a.m. on New Year's Day, staff from Memory Care called to tell me that Mother had fallen, and they did not know how long she had been lying on the floor. They had transferred her to a local hospital. The caller then said Mother would probably be alright, but that I could go to the hospital if I wanted to. Of course, I wanted to! I had been expecting something to happen—not this, but something. Mother's situation had deteriorated so much in the last few months.

It took me 30 minutes to dress and drive to the emergency room. I was ushered straight to her room and found a battered woman lying in the bed. No one was there with her. She had a white pad on her forehead above her red, swollen left eye and cheek. She had a serious cut on her left hand that had bled onto her pajama pants. The nurse had had to cut off her gown to get to her injuries. Mother's left shoulder had a large, red hematoma. Mother was awake and called my name. She said she was not in too much pain (I did not see how that could be), but that she was cold.

Around 4 a.m., the emergency room doctor came in. He examined Mother slowly and methodically. Only then did I see the open gash on her forehead. "That will need stitches," the doctor said. He had to move the blankets and Mother's arms to check her out. Mother complained of hurting during the examination. He ordered x-rays for her shoulder and left hand and tests for head and neck injuries. Mother did not appear to have injuries on her right side or her legs. After the doctor completed the exam, Mother allowed she was not in too much pain.

I had gotten Mother some extra blankets and had asked for a cup of coffee for me. The nurse adjusted the thermostat to make the room warmer. Two technicians came soon after the doctor's visit and took Mother for tests. I sat in a chair in her room and drifted off to sleep.

About 5 a.m., the technicians brought Mother back into her room. One said Mother moaned when moved but mostly slept through the tests. She moaned and spoke unintelligibly again in the room. She was cold, so I fetched her two more warm blankets. She became more restful and slept.

At 6:15, the doctor returned to report that despite Mother's cuts and bruises, she had no broken bones. In addition, the head exam did not show any trauma or bleeding, but her neck was bruised and likely she had strained ligaments, the doctor said. Five minutes later, someone came in and stitched up Mother's forehead with five stitches. The nurse bandaged the cut on Mother's left hand with Steri Strips and antibiotic gel. This activity got Mother's attention, and she complained as the nurse bandaged her wound, begging her to stop at one point.

After all the stitching and bandaging, Mother and I talked for a bit. I told her she had fallen and asked if she remembered doing so. Mother said she remembered stumbling but was not sure of a fall. Then she slept, but with some unintelligible talking. The staff wrapped Mother tightly in blankets for her trip back home. I drove back to Memory Care and met Mother and the ambulance drivers when they brought her back into her room. I could not do anything, so at 9:30 a.m. I left to go home.

Shortly after I arrived home, I received a call from the home health care service about meeting them that morning at Memory Care to discuss what they would do about Mother's leg wounds caused by the swelling. The nurse gave me their schedule for working on the wounds. After I explained about Mother's fall, the nurse said they would care for the hand wound, too, and watch for other signs arising from the fall. For now, the home health nurses would visit every other day.

I had hoped to learn more about what happened to Mother the night she fell, but the staff that came on at 7 a.m. that Sunday did not know much. It was Tuesday before I could talk with the head nurse. She was well aware of Mother's fall and said the alarm buzzer had alerted the staff right away. The nurse was not sure if Mother fell getting out of bed or if she just rolled off the bed. She also said that a report would have to be filed with the state. I knew it would be a big deal.

As I visited Mother over the next few days, I was amazed again at her. She looked terribly bruised, but she said she did not hurt anywhere. I don't know if she remembered the fall. As I recalled these memorable events that started the year, I went over in my mind what it meant. First, it meant Mother's bones were strong! Second, there was a procedure in place for an event such as this, and it worked well. Mother was well taken care of, even though she was alone in the emergency room. In fact, I did not *need* to be there, but I am pleased that I was.

The hospital care was relatively quick and efficient, and all of the admittance forms and insurance documents were taken care of by someone else. Mother was patched up and back home in Memory Care within six hours. She had survived a fall at near 98 years of age without too much damage. What a start to the year!

Happy Birthday, Number 98!

After an eventful start to the year, Mother continued to heal with a lessening of blue to her face and eye. In fact, she recovered much better than I expected. On Sunday, January 29th, a brother, my wife, and I celebrated with Mother her 98th birthday. After talking with the nurses, we decided not to have a Memory Care-wide party for the first time.

We brought Mother some gifts, including a blue gown that "looked like Mother." After the gifts were given, I asked her if she wanted some cake. I had bought Mother a small, single piece of decadent chocolate cake from the bakery. We put big "9" and "8" candles on the top, the slice being barely large enough to fit the candles. None of us wanted cake, and I fed Mother about half the piece. She enjoyed every mouthful, just as she always had done on her birthdays in Memory Care. She was awake for the party but soon slept after the activities finished. It was a good day—a good birthday, in fact, a great 98th birthday.

As I visited with Mother two or three times each week during January, it occurred to me that our conversations had once again changed. She was now wheelchair-bound, and I usually sat with her in the TV room or the activities room. There was little, if any, real talk. Mother slept restlessly much of the time, often sleeping and then opening her eyes. I hated that we could not talk anymore. On Mother's worst days, I had to get her attention to ask her if she hurt anywhere, or if she had slept well the night before, or one of my other common questions. Mother seemed to be far away, not hearing me until I repeated my question. She tuned out. After her short answer, she tuned out again. This was mostly the way of conversation now.

Not Public Food

Mother was quite surprising on my visit on Valentine's Day. Actually, our visit had nothing to do with Valentine's Day, and in fact I did not even bring it up. All the pink, heart-shaped decorations did not connect with her. Instead, the topic of the day was … food.

Mother started in on the topic right after she asked me "how I found her." She announced that some people had eaten "there" that morning. "There" was the activities room where the residents gathered to hear gospel music on the CD player and have a morning snack. At first Mother denied that she had had a snack but then remembered that she had. It was difficult for her to get the words out, but with some help and suggestions it seemed that she had eaten a cup of yogurt earlier.

But that little cup did not suffice. I asked her if she had eaten breakfast, and she allowed that she had. Mother was the most loquacious she had been in months, which led to a lively morning. She did not sleep. Along with her talkativeness about food, she also talked about "*your* dad," as she usually referred to my dad or her husband.

"Did your dad come with you?" Mother asked.

Without elaborating, I responded that he had not.

The subject of food, or a plate of food, quickly surfaced in the conversation again. Mother was sure that she would like to have a plate of food. Many people there were eating, she allowed more than once, with the strong suggestion that she was not. She was hungry.

"Are you okay to wait a few minutes? They are preparing lunch," I told her.

"I am not ravenous," she said.

But I was not convinced that she wasn't ravenous, and the talk of food did not lessen "They are fixing lunch," I said "and it will not be long. Can you wait?"

"Will they do that?" Mother asked, incredulously. She had no memory of the dining hall or the food preparation. I am not sure where she thought the food came from, or if she even thought about it at all. Often, she reverted back to thinking that she had cooked it.

"Your dad had this plate of food, and they said it was for him," Mother announced. "I did not take it. It was not public food."

Public food? I had not heard that term before, at least not used in that way. Perhaps Mother was thinking that there was "restricted food" and there was "public food." The staff would often bring their own food into the activities room for their lunch, or else eat while standing in the kitchen. Was this the other, "non-public" food Mother was thinking about?

I excused myself for a moment because Mother was so focused on food that I found it hard to talk with her, which was a shame since this was the first good conversation we had had in a while. I went to the office and talked to the staff. They said Mother ate well and often. One staff member had noticed Mother in the activities room and said how she licked her fingers at mealtime, just like she was doing then. Mother and her love of food were well known by all. Nurse Alicia allowed that she thought Mother just liked to eat, whether hungry or not. We agreed that she probably had no sense of satiety. It was similar to what Gina had mentioned earlier, that there was not enough food to fill Mother up.

When I returned, Mother and the others were being wheeled into the dining room. I offered to help since the line of three wheelchairs was a little cumbersome for one worker to handle. I pushed Mother to her place in the dining room and said I had to leave.

"Why do you have to go?" Mother inquired, as a worker placed a new bib around her neck.

"I have some things to do," I answered obliquely. I told her goodbye and hoped they had enough public food that day.

"I Have Got To Get Ready To Go"

Mother continued to have good days and not-so-good days, and all of us were amazed that she had seemed to plateau mentally and was in good spirits and often happy. However, the nurse telling me immediately upon my arrival that Mother "was active today" was a bad omen. Right away, Mother had started in about having to get dressed to go to … (she could not remember where). Mother then said she thought it was church they were going to. She was amazing in the detail of her plans. I asked her if the meeting at church was a reunion. She allowed that she thought it was a reunion of her folks. I asked her what she had prepared.

"Well," Mother began, "I cooked some sausage patties and got some rolls. Then I made a cake, or sort of a cake." She stammered a lot telling me about the foods.

"What kind of cake?" I asked next. "Was it your coconut cake?"

"No," she said, taking a long time to answer. "It wasn't coconut. It was a … peanut butter cake. I hope everyone will like it," she added.

Other than the peanut butter cake, everything sounded so normal, just like Mother had done many other times. The plan was clear in her mind. She even asked if Lilly was ready, making me think that this was, indeed, her family reunion.

Mother continued fretting over getting ready to go. She needed other clothes; she needed make-up; she needed her hair fixed. Today, she was persistent. I took her to her room thinking that would interrupt her thoughts, but it did not. In fact, she was going to get ready to go with or without my help. I took her back to the dining room and parked her with the other ladies again. I told them I could do nothing with her today. The nurse said that was why she had been in the dining room—so they could watch her. I feared she would get out of her seat. They said they would do all they could for her. I left without speaking to her again.

"She's a Fighter"

By mid-May, Mother's good days were becoming more confused, and she was having difficulty getting her thoughts together or her words out. I struggled with knowing how to join in the conversation at times. She would often say something involving "Danny," but without knowing I was next to her. She talked a lot about "him" today, and I pressed her on who she meant. Finally, she said a long-deceased first cousin of mine. When Alicia asked who was with her today (meaning me), Mother really fumbled, talking about another first cousin and others, but never getting to my name. I finally said I was Dan, her youngest. She agreed.

Alicia and I discussed Mother's sores, the swelling in her legs, and that she was losing her ability to feed herself. Alicia mentioned getting a hospital bed and its value in preventing bruising to Mother's arms and in allowing workers to raise Mother's legs to alleviate the swelling. Alicia also thought it was time to look into hospice care again. We agreed that Mother had a habit of "rising to the occasion" when new folks visited—which, Alicia said, was exactly what had happened the last time the doctor interviewed Mother for hospice. She had not spoken two words all day, but as soon as the doctor showed up, Mother became the gracious, chatty host, even inviting the doctor to dinner. As such, he did not see someone in need of hospice care but someone active with dementia. Alicia said she would talk to the doctor about this.

Then, Alicia indicated that Mother was slipping: She could not feed herself; she had swelling and sores; she could be feisty sometimes and at other times docile. "The other day, she just looked different," said Alicia, "but the next day it was back to normal." Mother wouldn't give up. As Alicia remarked, "She's a fighter." Amen to that!

What Can We Do?

Mother continued in much the same way for several weeks in May and June. The sores on her legs got better, thanks to the home health nurses who came every week. But other sores developed, and a particular one on her right foot was very painful and perhaps infected. Further, Mother had bouts when she hardly moved but slept very hard. The staff told me that at times she was very talkative, but I had not witnessed that in the past couple of weeks. In fact, Alicia had put Mother on the sofa in the TV room to get her feet up. (Mother did not like to stay isolated in her room.) When I arrived to visit, Mother was fast asleep with her mouth opened. Her face was thin and ashen. She looked dead, and I watched intently for a while to be sure she was breathing. Alicia shared the same concern and gently shook Mother until she woke up.

"Ughh!" Mother groaned, 'Why are you waking me?"

Mother's new doctor and Alicia were planning to get the hospital bed. Although Mother had flunked getting into hospice care, this doctor planned to try again. Her condition was obviously worsening, and there was nothing we could do but wait.

Notes

[1]David Schenk, *The Forgetting: Alzheimer's: Portrait of an Epidemic* (New York: Anchor, 2003).

[2]James VanOosting, "The Last Bursts of Memory," in *The American Scholar* (Winter, 2017), 87–91.

[3]Kate Atkinson, *Behind the Scenes at the Museum* (New York: Picador, 1955), 320–321.

[4]John Swinton, *Dementia: Living in the Memories of God* (Eerdmans Publishing Co., Grand Rapids, 2012). [5]Frederick A. Trunk, *Alzheimer's/Dementia from the Experiences of a Caregiver* (Xulon Press, U.S. [self-published], 2012).

"Mrs. Akin was an extremely special resident to me. Like with our children, I know we should not have favorites, but she always held a special place in my heart. I too have three sons, so she and I made that connection as soon as I started at HHV. She was one of the sweetest souls you could ever meet."

—Tanya Adcock, Director of St. Mary's Health Care System, Highland Hills Village, sitting with Mother

Chapter 4
Hospice Care

While Mother had previously "flunked" being accepted into home hospice care, by June she had declined enough physically and mentally to "pass" and be admitted to the program. I met with the coordinator and the nurse who would evaluate Mother's condition. The nurse was the same one who had evaluated Mother for hospice the previous December. We went through the same interview process as before, and the nurse acknowledged that she could see a steep decline in Mother since that last meeting. It was hard to get her awake, and when she was, she did not give a logical response to the nurse's question. The decline in Mother's cognitive skills, her much-reduced ability to walk due to the foot sores, and her inability to feed herself did it for Mother this time.

Mother did not have to physically move; the program came to her. Everything would be the same for Mother but with the advantage of extra assistance, care, and attention in her room in Memory Care. This program would be the same as if she lived in her own home. I had a long talk with the hospice coordinator and the nurse about Mother. I put to them the question of where she was on a timeline for dementia patients—I was hopeful that from their experience I might gain some information on what to expect. They saw Mother going downhill, and even though hospice expects death within six months, they still asked about resuscitation and whether a funeral home had been chosen. They were preparing.

The booklet provided by hospice was informative on the signs of impending death. The first sign was a change in body temperature, with feet and hands becoming bluish, and the face becoming gray. Mother's hands and feet had been blue for some time, but the ashen gray appearance of her face a few days earlier was different. Another sign was increasing sleep with unresponsiveness. Mother had shown this a few weeks back when she seemed to sleep most of the day. Disorientation was another sign. Although Mother did have some of the signs, she lacked others and had normal breathing and a good appetite.

Mother's home hospice care program would follow a specific routine: About once a week a nurse would coordinate with the Memory Care staff and direct the aides to assist with bathing, eating, and whatever else was needed. Home health care would be suspended and hospice would take over the care of Mother's sores, provide incontinence supplies, and bring a hospital bed. Hospice would also take care of tests for UTIs and other things. I arranged to donate Mother's own bed, which had been with her forever it seemed, to a local charity for homeless families.

The medicine Abilify, which is prescribed for mood disorders, had already been reduced for Mother from 5 mg to 2.5 mg in June with no ill effects. I asked hospice to talk to Mother's doctor about reducing her other medicines, especially any that were prescribed just to keep her alive. Her Exelon patch, prescribed solely to Alzheimer's sufferers, was discontinued in mid-June, and other medicines were dropped later.

After the hospice coordinator had gone over the details of Mother's new care procedures, she asked me what I wanted for Mother. I told her that I wanted Mother to live pain-free. I thought later that I should have added, "and to live where she *is now* for the duration." I told Nurse Alicia about this conversation and added the two things that I wanted for Mother; Alicia said that is what she wanted, too.

A Visit With My Brothers

A few days after Mother went under hospice care, my two brothers came for a visit. I had tried to prepare them for a big change in Mother since they had last seen her, but they reported that she was really "with it" and they had a great visit. When asked if she liked her new (hospital) bed, Mother had said she did, but that she liked the old one too.

Two things stuck out to me from the report of my brothers' visit: First, Mother could still rise to the occasion and be a gracious host. Second, she was aware that she had a new bed (unless, perhaps, she picked up on the fact that my brothers talked about a new bed and she played along). It has been noted that people in Mother's condition can often detect in a person's voice something that cues them to give the "correct" answer. I wondered what Mother would have said if they had asked if she liked her bed, without specifying "new." Earlier, I had simply asked her if she had slept well, and she always said yes, without any mention of her bed … old or new.

All in all, Mother seemed to be okay with the hospital bed, and life went on. She continued to sleep a lot, but not as much since the doctor changed her medication. Sometimes she said she wanted to go home (a request I had not heard for a while), and once she asked a resident seated next to her—and in much the same condition—if she was ready to go. Other times, she said it must be a pretty day (it was raining cats and dogs) because everyone had stayed home from work. The TV room was full of folks, and maybe that was the cause for the remark. So far, Alicia and I had our wish: Mother seemed pain-free and was still at home in Memory Care.

Hospice Healing

After a month in hospice care, Mother was remarkably alert. I had noticed during my last several visits—and staff reports verified this—that her alertness had improved. For the first time in months, she mentioned the Lord and his taking care of her. We had a nice conversation, not deep but nice, for the first time in a while. But after 10 or 15 minutes, she fell asleep. I took the opportunity to speak to Nurse Alicia about Mother.

"It's just my term," Alicia allowed, "but I call it 'hospice healing.'" She said that Mother's improved alertness could be related to changes in her medication, but she had seen "hospice healing" over and over again. Alicia volunteered that it might be due to more attention and care from additional nurses and from having more visits from family, but it was common.

I also learned that "hospice healing" comes before a decline. I asked Alicia if the expected decline would take Mother to where she was before the improvement, or would it take her even lower. Alicia said it was not possible to know. She indicated that Mother's decline over time had been slow, and she gave me the impression that Mother's expected decline after "hospice healing" would also be slow. But no one knew for sure.

"Do You Know Who I Am?"

In the last week of July, Mother seemed to be less "healed." On our way to the dining room after a good conversation, she asked me, "Do you know who I am?"

Without any great surprise or hesitation, I told her I did indeed know who she was. Then I asked her, "Do you know who I am?"

"No, I don't think I do."

I told her I was Dan, her youngest son. Mother said she did remember me then. A few days later she had forgotten me again, but later seemed to remember. She continued to think about food and family, and these two subjects were often intertwined. On the last Saturday in July, Mother told me a story. "We all had breakfast together. Then we went down to the barn. The cow was having a calf," Mother said, as if she remembered it precisely. I could not discern if she was back at her growing-up home or was visiting with Aunt Lilly, who also had a farm. But Mother was smiling the whole time, indicating that it was a pleasant visit.

That day the nurse agreed that Mother was returning to normal after a brief stint of "hospice healing." I asked her for a copy of Mother's medicines since the pharmacy bill was very low and only included medicines for half the month. The hospice doctor had dropped the Namenda along with some others, agreeing that Mother was beyond the need for such medicines now.

She was still doing remarkably well for $98^{1/2}$ years old. I was feeling better about Mother, too. I noticed that she had a lot of incontinent pants, and the hospice nurses were doing their job taking care of her. With hospice taking over Mother's care, I could now just visit with her, putting a blanket over her if she was cold, and talking to her as much as she wished. She seemed pain-free and was at "her home."

Alicia and Mother

Nurse Alicia glanced up and gave me a pleasant look. As always, she was very busy attending to what was needed—and at this time it was lunch. "I'm going to let you take her back out," Alicia said about Mother, adding, "She is not very happy with me right now."

It was clear that Mother and Alicia had locked horns, again. Alicia and the other staff members went out of their way to please the residents' visitors. I guess they thought we would complain if they didn't, but later events convinced me that pleasing others was Alicia's nature. From my perspective, Alicia and the staff did an excellent job of caring for Mother and showed her love and respect all the time, even under difficult times, such as today!

Alicia continued talking as I was taking Mother back to her room, "She was hungry, and I had given her a yogurt cup. She ate it all and wanted more. She broke the plastic spoon and was about to eat that. We didn't want that or we would have more problems." Then she added, "She said she wished I would quit getting in her way!"

The way that Alicia relayed the story indicated that Mother was angry. Alicia was laughing and said how much she loved Mother, but I thought I detected a bit of hurt feelings. As she hurried to get lunch ready, Alicia encountered at least one contrary person (and maybe more). She was also trying to explain to a son why his mother was unhappy with her. Mother heard Alicia explaining the situation as we moved to her room. Then, she began to give her side of it.

"I think one of the mothers had some trouble getting lunch ready," Mother said, aware there had been a dust-up. Back in her room, she commented on how well *their* room looked, not realizing it was *her* room. I moved her wheelchair to a wide place in the room and put my fold-up chair next to her.

"Mother," I started, "do you know who I am?" She did not.

"I am Dan, your youngest son."

"So, you're the other Dan," Mother said with a smile. Perhaps she remembered enough to know that a Dan visited her, but she didn't know me.

So, I replied with emphasis, "I am *the* Dan."

She tried to say something that began with a "b"—perhaps "one of the brothers" or "brood"—but the word would not come out. I told her that her oldest son had visited her the previous week, and that the week before that her other son had also visited. I told her that he liked to paint and that she had some of his paintings up on her walls. She never looked around to see them. In fact, she just silently stared off to the side as if she had tuned me out. I thought she had not heard me or had fallen asleep with her eyes open. But after some moments had passed, she spoke.

"He always was a better painter than the others."

I agreed and added that he was the only one who had any artistic ability among us. Then, I told her that she and I had had a conversation some time ago about talent and that she had artistic talent in sewing. Mother smiled again and agreed that she could sew. I asked her if she learned to sew from her mother; she said she had.

"Mother would take in clothes and sew in her home," Mother said. This statement implied that Grandmother sewed for others and perhaps for payment, so I asked about it. "No. She just sewed for the family," replied Mother. "She is not doing that much anymore." While Mother had forgotten that Grandmother had died in 1953, she seemed to be clear on the things that had happened back then.

I thought Mother looked different today. I studied her carefully for details: Her face was not as thin but, in fact, seemed a bit fleshier today. Her eyes were clear. There was no redness or watering of her eyes as there had been so often. Her hair was light gray (not white or silver), thin, and just messy enough to be cute. She did not look bedraggled at all. But there were places on her hands and fingers that were dark, dark blue.

I told her, "Your hair is fine and like mine, almost the same color." Then I added, "Some folks say we look alike."

Mother smiled and replied, "We're related."

On two occasions, Mother said something about the little boy with me or about the baby "over there." There was a clock on the windowsill that may have looked like a boy's face to her, and an artificial flower might have resembled a baby. She had said similar things in the past about inanimate objects. I did not know if she was hallucinating or just not seeing reality.

About 10 minutes to noon, I took Mother back to the dining room, put her bib on, and told her she had water and tea. Thank goodness there was something there for her, even if it was just liquid. I assured her food was coming soon. She seemed more concerned at this moment about how she would do things, so I assured her that the folks there would take care of her.

"Have you talked to them about it?" she asked.

I told her I had and that they knew everything they were supposed to do. I told her I had to go but that I would see her again soon. She wanted to know more about when that might be, but I was able to convince her that I would see her soon. She thanked me for coming and seemed to be okay.

A Fine Routine

Mother was once again in the recliner chair in the TV room, covered with a blanket and sound asleep at 11 a.m. The staff said they would put her there after breakfast (maybe often) and she would sleep until lunch. Alicia allowed that Mother did not like to stay in her room but liked the ancillary noise. Since Mother's lift chair was never used, I offered it to Alicia to put in the common room if they needed it.

As I sat next to her, Mother opened her eyes and saw me. I told her good morning, and she said something like, "Hello, darling." I asked if she knew who I was. She said yes but called me by my older brother's name, and then Dan. It was like old times when Mother would go through the list of her boys to get to me. After we talked a bit, she fell asleep again and I left.

"A Change in Residence Is Important"

The September visit with Mother harkened to past times when we sat and visited in her independent living apartment. Today, she was listening to gospel music on the CD player in the activities room, and seemed to be asleep when I arrived. She was pleasant and insightful.

"Your great-granddaughter is beginning to look at colleges," I said. "Before long she will be leaving home."

"A change in residence is an important time," Mother confirmed.

She was good today, and alert when she was not dozing. As usual, Mother was happy when the staff arrived to take her to lunch—and then she would easily let me go.

"Just Live"

Mother declined from a few weeks back. She seemed out of it much of the time. The last visit had not been a good one. She was intently fondling the puzzle in front of her, which was already put together. She teased a piece off the puzzle, held it, and then tried to put it in her mouth.

"Mother, that is not food," I said. "It is cardboard. It would not be good for you to eat." She did not eat the piece but instead said something about it not being chicken, or knowing it was cardboard. In her mind, Mother still wanted something to eat, and it seemed like it was chicken that she wanted. I took her to the dining room where the workers were preparing lunch. I put a bib on her and, when she appeared to doze, left.

Alicia said Mother would be evaluated for continuation in the hospice program. Mother had to be declining—not staying the same but *declining*—to stay in the program. Alicia said it would be their call. I thought, how can anyone think Mother is *not* declining?

I thought of Mother on a Monday near the end of September. We had held a funeral at the church for a 17-year-old high school junior. During the solemn service, the preacher had read a scripture passage from Jeremiah 29:1-14 about how the southern kingdom of Israel was overrun by the Babylonians and how many people were captured and taken to Babylon. The message of Jeremiah—and the message of the preacher—was to accept that when bad things happen that you cannot change, you should continue to do what you have always done. Jeremiah said to marry, have children, till the soil, and eat the produce of your gardens. When things happen and you cannot change them, continue to do what you have always done. I could not help but think of Mother's similar, but simpler, philosophy: "Just live."

Mother Sings

Mother was sitting in the activities room on Thursday, the first week of October, surrounded by others who were also listening to old songs being played on an audiocassette player. The songs were familiar, and Mother said that she "was enjoying the music." She was smiling. As she and I talked and then sat silent as she appeared to doze, I thought I heard her humming the tune. Surely not. Probably the lady *next* to Mother was humming. Then the staff moved the lady, leaving just Mother and me. Mother *was* humming, and nodding her head, and then singing words!

"Its a Grand Old Flag" was the first song I heard her humming. She also nodded her head in tune with "Yankee Doodle Dandy," then sang out the words to "Polly Wolly Doodle All The Day." Alicia and others said she had been singing that morning. It was a good day.

We Are Lost to Her Pretty Much

Two days later, I visited Mother just about the time the workers were taking her to the bathroom. I said I would wait in her room. Mother was rolled out of the bathroom, smiling and happy to see me—or any visitor. She looked good, with her hair fixed and all smiles. Her face looked fuller. It was not as swollen and frail as it had been recently. I felt Mother's hands and said she felt warm, although she said she was cold. I asked her if she wanted a blanket. I never got a clear answer, so I picked up a colorful fleece throw from her chair and put it over her. I had never seen this throw before, as was the case with many of the things Mother had acquired. On the other hand, I had not seen Mother's own blankets in a while. It is called "communal living," I think.

"That feels good," Mother replied when I wrapped the throw around her. Even though she smiled at me, her look caused me to wonder if she knew who I was.

"Mother, do you know who I am?" I asked fearfully.

She thought for a moment and then replied, "Samuel …" I think she was about to say something else, but I interrupted her and said, "I am Dan."

"What?" Mother replied.

"I am Dan, your youngest son." I repeated.

"Oh yeah. Dan," Mother acknowledged.

"You know you have two other sons," I continued. "Do you know their names?" Getting no answer, I jumped in again and told her. Then she added, "They are singing today."

Mother dozed off and on. At some point, we got onto the subject of work and the need to work. "My husband has things to do," Mother said. It was interesting that she used the term "her husband" rather than "your dad." I think this was another indication she did not know who I was.

It was Saturday in early October. Mother was $98^{3/4}$ years old now. As the new year rolled around, she declined, with bad days and better (but not good) days. The bad days meant deep sleep in the recliner in the TV room without ever awakening while I was there, or lack of recognition of me on visits. The better days were short periods of shallow conversation, often asking about one of the relatives on her or Dad's side of the family. Soon after our conversations, she would take a short nap. At times she was clingy when I said I needed to leave, and at other times she let me go with ease. When I visited, the workers (all women at this time) would come over and talk to Mother and love on her. Mother got along with all of them, and everyone was very kind to her.

I wondered if there a way to get some support for Mother's head as she slept upright in her wheelchair. We bought an "airline pillow" for support so she would not have to hold her head up all the time. Then one day I noticed Mother had a high-back wheelchair where she could lean back and have full support of her head. Her legs were too short for the footrests, so pads were ordered, and Mother could touch "the bottom" now. While she still slumped at times, a quick jerk up by two of the workers remedied that position, and she seemed to sit better … after the shock of being jerked up! But Mother adapted to the new wheelchair and told me later that "she liked the new chair."

Gina and Alicia had both eased my concerns by saying that the plan was to look after Mother for as long as it took. Home hospice made that possibility real. Even so, Mother seemed tired of being there, although this is just my perspective as she always said that she was okay. She rarely complained, but it must have been hard for her.

Chapter 5
Going Home

Nurse Alicia called me at 9 a.m. on the first Friday in March, one day after Mother's seventh anniversary in Memory Care. "There's no emergency," she began. But then she told me that they had put Mother on oxygen Thursday evening, and she was not able to swallow well and had refused her meal. Fluid was building up in her lungs and chest. Hospice had begun morphine treatment on Thursday evening as well. It took a while for me to realize what Nurse Alicia was actually saying.

"Are you saying we are in the last times for Mother?" I asked.

Alicia responded with a soft, weepy, "Yes." She then said it could be hours or days—up to a couple of weeks before Mother died. There was just no way to predict a time. Along with giving Mother oxygen and morphine, hospice had orders to withhold all food and water. Mother was dying.

"Should I call my brothers to come over?" I asked.

"I think I would," Alicia said.

While I admit Mother's death was expected, it was not expected *now*. I called my brothers and told them, "If you want to see Mother alive once more, you should plan to come over soon," and they did. They made 90-minute trip together that Friday morning, and I met them when they arrived at noon. We were all in Mother's room, and she was in her bed covered with one of her best quilts. The nurses had told us that we should talk and let Mother hear our voices because she could still hear us even though there might not be a response.

As we talked, Mother began kicking vigorously under the covers. I can only guess that she was trying to communicate with us, letting us know that she was aware we were all there, and maybe even trying to get into the conversation. We stayed a while, then came to my home for lunch. The brothers returned to see Mother again before leaving for their homes.

Mother did not die within hours; instead, she lasted another week. As she lay in her bed covered with a blanket and a quilt, she was mostly still. At times, her eyes would pop open, and she would stare straight ahead. I, and others there, would talk to her and tell her we loved her. At times, she would leave her eyes open for a while and even try to speak.

The preacher came over soon after I called him. He visited Mother and those of us with her for three days straight. On his first visit to Mother, she was responding only slightly with light moans and the irregular opening of her eyes. With the preacher close by talking to her, Mother mustered all her energy and yelled, "Get away from me!" Then she repeated it again, "Get away from me!"

Everyone was shocked, and I could not make out why this had happened. The preacher, I am sure, was also surprised by the outburst but nonplussed. He backed away and said to

Mother, "Is this far enough?" She did not respond again but closed her eyes and seemed to go to sleep. The only explanation I have for Mother's unusual behavior was that the preacher was too loud or that he was not a son. To his credit, the preacher came and visited and ministered to all of us many more times.

The Memory Care staff said they would not move Mother up the hill to the hospice house but would keep her where she was until the end. Mother was in the room she had occupied for seven years. After a day or so, it was clear that she would remain alive for more than a few hours. My wife encouraged me to stay with Mother a lot, remembering her own times with her mother a few years back. She sat with me during much of this early watch. While we stayed late in the evenings, we left for the night when the morphine, Haldol, and Ativan had done their job to relax and calm Mother.

I read the book *Final Gifts*,[1] where nurses told of the last moments of their patients when they made unusual requests or spoke words as they were dying and "[meeting] someone to take them over." I read how the dying would often wait until a loved one came into their room or left the room before they died. It was as if they chose the time to die—"a final gift" to their loved ones. At one point, Mother appeared to reach out her arms like she was trying to touch or grab something. The nurses said that was not unusual, but I tried to see more in her reaching and in her opening her eyes and staring at the ceiling.

I took some work material for the church history book I was writing and tried to look through materials as I sat with Mother. The early mornings, when I was there in Mother's room with just her and me were blessed times. I thought, I am with Mother, who is resting comfortably in her last hours. I do not have to sit in a hospital and deal with all that. I am with Mother in her room for the final hours. She is resting. She is at peace. I am at peace.

On Tuesday or Wednesday (I cannot remember which), Mother had a rough afternoon. Her breathing was deep and labored, and it seemed she struggled to get a breath. She was gurgling with each breath. At times, it was easier for her, but the deep breathing and gurgling would start again. The nurses were quick to respond, usually by shifting Mother's head to open the air passage and by giving her more morphine, Haldol, and Ativan. Afterward, Mother seemed to relax. I stayed later that night until she seemed to be resting.

On Thursday, a brother came to visit again. We visited in Mother's room, talking as usual and trying *not* to be quiet. We wanted her to hear us, to know we were there, and to respond if she could. A granddaughter also came over briefly to see her grandmother that afternoon. My brother and I stayed with Mother until about 7 o'clock that evening. It seemed as though she was resting and it would be another night of waiting. My brother left for home. I went to Mother's bedside and touched her and told her I loved her. Harking back to stories in *Final Gifts*, I told her, "It is okay for you to go, Mother. We are all okay."

I thought about leaving my church history materials in Mother's room since I would be there early the next morning, but I reconsidered and decided to gather up my materials. I left for home. Supper was waiting, and a few minutes after arriving home, I sat down to eat.

My cell phone rang, but as was our usual practice we did not answer a name or number we did not recognize. Immediately afterward, however, the home phone rang. I thought I should answer.

"Dan," the weekday nurse Kathleen said, "Your mother just passed away."

Even though I expected it, I did not expect it *now*. Kathleen said Mother had died 10 or 15 minutes earlier, about 7:15 p.m. She and another worker, April, were present.

Kathleen said, "She took two deep breaths and then died," then told me that the hospice nurse would come by in about 45 minutes to pronounce death.

I called both my brothers. I tried to eat but could not. My wife finished the few bites left on her plate, and we headed to Memory Care. Mother was in the bed. She was still warm, and her countenance was much as I had seen it many times that week. I looked at her for a while, thinking that her long battle was over. She was at peace. And while it would be more than presumptuous for me to say I know, I can say I hope—I believe—that she was in a better place and with Dad and her mother.

We waited for the hospice nurse to come and pronounce death. When she arrived, she held her stethoscope on Mother's chest and waited, then moved the stethoscope to near the carotid artery and waited some more. I did not speak while the nurse listened and stared at her watch. The nurse pronounced Mother's death at 8:09 p.m. on March 8. The nurse then asked us to leave for a moment while she did some cleaning up. She called the ambulance to take Mother to the funeral home.

As Mother lay dead on the bed, my mind went to Jesus and how much worse his death must have been than the peaceful one Mother had experienced. Then my mind turned to the Resurrection. And now Mother had finally realized the hope that she had so often expressed: She was going home.

Note

[1] M. Callanan and P. Kelley, *Final Gifts* (New York: Simon and Shuster, 1992).